Yes, Miss Gibson

JAMES AITCHISON & REG JAMES

The life and times of an Australian radio legend

Copyright © 2014 James Aitchison & Reg James

Published by Vivid Publishing
P.O. Box 948, Fremantle
Western Australia 6959
www.vividpublishing.com.au

National Library of Australia Cataloguing-in-Publication data:
Creator: Aitchison, Jim, author.
Title: Yes, Miss Gibson : the life and times of an Australian radio legend /
           James Aitchison, Reg James.
ISBN: 9781925209167 (paperback)
Subjects: Gibson, Grace I., OAM (Grace Isabel), 1905-1989.
           Radio producers and directors--Australia--Biography.
           Radio--Production and direction--Australia--History.
Other Creators/Contributors:
           James, Reg, author.
Dewey Number: 791.440232092

Photographs courtesy of Grace Gibson company archives, and from author's collection and sources. If a credit has been overlooked, apologies are offered, and upon notification any omission will be rectified at the first opportunity.

All rights reserved. No part of this publication may be reproduced, stored in a retrieval system or transmitted in any form or by any means, electronic, mechanical, photocopying, recording or otherwise, without the prior written permission of the copyright owner. The information, views, opinions and visuals expressed in this publication are solely those of the author and do not reflect those of the publisher. The publisher disclaims any liabilities or responsibilities whatsoever for any damages, libel or liabilities arising directly or indirectly from the contents of this publication.

Contents

Episode 1: Amazing Grace 7
We meet Grace Gibson, a girl from El Paso, and follow her early life in Hollywood. The chapter explores the pioneering days of American and Australian radio drama, setting the context for Grace's arrival in Sydney

Episode 2: The man from Shanghai 19
Grace becomes the highest paid woman in prewar Australian radio. We trace her friendship with Frank Packer, how she gained a husband, and opened her own production company

Episode 3: "A Grace Gibson Radio Production" 28
Against fierce opposition, Grace's first postwar radio dramas set a new standard. We discover how these early shows were recorded and distributed on huge transcription discs

Episode 4: Golden age, Midas touch 40
We explore radio's importance in postwar Australian society. In an age of innocence, radio was the local "Hollywood", and Grace quickly dominated its golden years

Episode 5: From soaps to spies 58
Grace launches her famous long-running soaps such as *Dr Paul*, and produces new shows like *Night Beat* and *Dossier on Dumetrius*, which are still being played today

Episode 6: The fabulous Fifties 79
Grace buys a new studio, captures global markets, and experiments with television drama

Episode 7: A cast of thousands 102
Sydney's radio industry worked at a frantic pace. Veterans such as Dinah Shearing, Alastair Duncan, and Michael Pate share memories of a bizarre acting fraternity where the glamour all too often concealed alcoholism

Episode 8: The plot thickens, the action quickens 125
Grace relied on the best writers such as Peter Yeldham and Ross Napier, who reflect on churning out thousands of pages of dialogue for an insatiable industry

Episode 9: Next stop, Hollywood 155
Grace's top stars such as Peter Finch, Michael Pate, and Rod Taylor find success in movies

Episode 10: The one-eyed monster 164
The arrival of television signaled the end of radio drama. Surprisingly though, the industry still flourished, only to be brought to its knees by the Top 40 radio format

Episode 11: The long good-bye 168
Radio production houses were closing. Grace survived, buying her competitors' programmes, expanding overseas markets, and switching to short-length dramas

Episode 12: And so ends our story 192
In 1982, Grace Gibson's newest, most successful radio drama, *Castlereagh Line*, was playing in every radio market in Australia. Seven years later, Grace died alone, leaving strict instructions who could attend her funeral

Episode 1
Amazing Grace

WHEN Grace Isabel Gibson was born on 17 June 1905 in El Paso, Texas, the daughter of rancher and taxi driver Calvin Newton Gibson, a card-carrying member of the Ku Klux Klan, there were no such things as radio stations. By the time she finished school, the new medium was already in its infancy. By late 1922, 560 American stations were on the air.

Grace was the third of four children. Bertha and Dora were the elder sisters. Calvin was her younger brother. Sometimes they lived on a farm. Other times they moved back into town.

El Paso was on the Mexican border, and, like her hometown, Grace was the product of two cultures on her mother's side. From Margaret Escobara, born in Mexico City, Grace could claim Mexican ancestry, as her heavy-lidded brown eyes and frequently impassive expression attested. Certainly, her penchant for spicy Mexican cuisine travelled with her all her life. Her mother also endowed her daughter with German blood from the Schultz family — a fact that "explained her Brunnhilde stature and untroubled air of taking business in her stride", as a Sydney reporter would later observe of Grace.

JUST weeks before Grace's seventh birthday, her destiny was shaped by an event that unfolded on 14 April on the other side of America. David

Sarnoff, a young telegraph operator at the Marconi station in New York, picked up a message from the North Atlantic: "RMS *Titanic* ran into iceberg, sinking fast." Sarnoff stayed at his post for the next 72 hours, broadcasting in Morse the world's first news of the disaster. The passionate Sarnoff climbed the ranks at the Marconi Company and in 1915 wrote a memo to the great inventor himself about a vision he had of a "radio music box" which could broadcast music into every American home. Marconi thought his idea crazy; in those days, shipping and amateur wireless enthusiasts used radio, but who would want to actually "listen" to it?

Marconi must have kicked himself. After the First World War, his American assets were absorbed into General Electric. The old Marconi Company became RCA and Sarnoff got the green light. "Radio music boxes" became radio receivers. Eventually RCA's National Broadcasting Company would dominate America's golden age of radio, with Sarnoff at the helm.

Grace was 15 when the first radio station in the world, KDKA Pittsburgh, went to air in 1920. Two years later Kolin Hager, programme director of WGY in Schenectady, New York, a General Electric station, invented radio drama. His concept was *One Man's Family*, which later became a major daytime serial on NBC until the 1960s. The first plays were broadcast "live", but from the late 1920s radio shows could be recorded on machines such as the Blattnerphone and the Marconi-Stille. Sound was recorded magnetically on rapidly spinning reels of steel wire. Editing was crude. By cutting the wire, any unwanted section could be removed before tying the ends together again.

The big breakthrough came in the early 1930s, when programmes were being "transcribed" onto wax discs from which a matrix could be made. Pressings were stamped from the matrix and distributed to hundreds of different radio stations. Technology had spawned a new industry. In February 1932 America invented the "soap opera" when

Colgate-Palmolive's Super Suds sponsored the first daytime serial on the NBC network. Not to be outdone, Procter & Gamble's Oxydol followed suit and a new genre was born. The transcription business had begun and with it came Grace's lifelong career. But not just yet…

LIFE in El Paso honed Grace's survival instincts. She'd been brought up hard and knew the meaning of a dollar.

Encircled by the mile-high Franklin Mountains, El Paso was named after a pass cut by the Rio Grande. Temperatures soar to 108 degrees Fahrenheit at the drop of a sombrero. Cotton, peanuts, beans and sorghum grow in the surrounding countryside. On the outskirts, a massive statue of the crucifixion atop the 4,576-ft Sierra de Cristo Rey marks the point where Mexico, Texas and New Mexico meet. This is the country where Pat Garrett shot Billy the Kid in 1881, and Pancho Villa's marauders raided the town of Columbus in 1916. Over the border in Ciudad Juarez, girls were still available for fifty cents.

Small wonder that Margaret Gibson counselled her daughters to get wise to the commercial world. They studied practical things at school like bookkeeping, shorthand and typing. Subjects like history weren't going to get them a decent living and a share of the American dream.

For all its faults, El Paso would always be home. Fifty years later Grace returned for visits, a local hero, the hometown girl made good. Her sister Dora and brother Calvin still lived there. Soft-spoken Calvin was a Will Rogers-type character who worked for the American Telephone Company virtually all his life. Her generosity to family members was boundless. Calvin and his wife were able to point out appliances in their home: "Grace bought that refrigerator the year before last … Grace got us that television set last year." (When a Gibson executive once paid them a visit with duty-free Scotch, they wrote and told Grace how generous he was. "What do you mean generous?" replied Grace. "He put it on his expenses.")

Grace finished high school in El Paso. Years after, at an office party in Sydney, she sang and danced her old high school song at two in the morning.

She skipped college and worked in a local bank, rising to the top of the typing pool. Along the way she learned a lot about money and certainly the care of it. Then, like thousands of other star-struck young American girls of the time, she followed Bertha and Dora to Hollywood. Any job she could get in the movies, she'd take.

Grace, ever one for a legend, liked to recount her experiences working at Central Casting. Australian newspaper reporters lapped it up. Her life in Hollywood was like a page from an F. Scott Fitzgerald novel. It was the Prohibition era, the Roaring 20s, a time when flappers danced the Blackbottom, and Grace smuggled hooch into parties under her fur coat. "I was quite gay then," she once remarked, "though not the way it's meant today!" By all accounts, she was the consummate party animal.

Somewhere along the line she got married.

Her first husband, Thomas Atchison, remains a mystery. There was some speculation that he was an American, and a singer, but probably not a very good one. As a friend later observed, "Although certain staff members knew of Grace's previous marriage, they considered it none of their business to ask. Also, there was too much respect for her second husband Ronnie Parr to show interest." In a bizarre coincidence, Grace's mother and her three daughters all married twice. Her mother was a Gibson, and then became a Wheelock; Bertha was first a Graves, then became a Watt; Dora married a Make, then a Sullivan.

Almost by accident, Grace stumbled into radio.

When the Radio Transcription Company of America opened its doors, it was one of the first studios to record radio dramas for syndication to stations around the United States. And Grace Gibson, errand girl, switchboard operator and two-fingered typist, was one of its first employees. Before long, her magnetic personality landed her the job of auditioning and selling the company's programmes to potential sponsors. Grace described it as "exactly the same as I did all through my life".

Business boomed for Grace in the depths of the Great Depression. By 1932 Americans had purchased close to 30 million radio sets. Listening to the radio was America's favourite nightly pastime. Radio was a cheap form of escape. A five-tube, mahogany-finished Silvertone radio receiver from Sears, Roebuck was $24.95 — four dollars down, with four-dollar monthly instalments.

Hollywood was the last boomtown, an oasis in a depressed America where one quarter of the labour force was out of work and out on the road. The fabulously rich still celebrated their wealth. Film stars and moguls filled their swimming pools with lotus blossoms and imported maple trees from Japan for a night of Oriental bacchanalia, then discarded them the next day as though the Roaring Twenties had never ended.

Then came 1933. And in the way that one of her serials might have unfolded, two men were poised to enter Grace's life and change it forever. One would bring her to Australia; the other would marry her there.

THE first man came from a background that couldn't have been more different to Hollywood: the urbane public accountant and former meatworks manager Alfred Edward Bennett, known to all as A. E. Bennett. A member of the Theosophical Society of Australia, he was managing director at its Sydney radio station, 2GB. Bennett believed that wireless should be utilized for "the Nation's uplift and progress". He also believed Australia needed strong leaders and openly admired Mussolini. Immersed in the work of the All for Australia League, he was defeated as a United Australia Party candidate in 1931. His elder brother was the controversial General Gordon Bennett, a highly decorated officer during World War I who is best remembered for his role in the Fall of Singapore; as commander of the Australian 8th

Division, he escaped before the surrender, leaving his men to become prisoners of the Japanese.

Despite his unlikely qualifications, A. E. Bennett was a shrewd broadcaster. He promoted many of radio's early stars such as the young New Zealand crooner Jack Davey, Charles Cousens, and Eric Colman, brother of Hollywood actor Ronald. He soon became the vigorous chief spokesman for Australia's fledgling broadcasters.

Australia's broadcasting industry was growing rapidly. The first Sydney station, 2SB, operated by Broadcasters (Sydney) Ltd., had gone on air at 8 p.m. on 23 November 1923 from a rooftop studio at the *Smith's Weekly* building. It was followed a fortnight later on 5 December 1923 by 2FC, operated by a department store, Farmer & Co. The 2SB call sign caused such confusion with 2FC that the owners obligingly changed it to 2BL. In 1924, 3AR Melbourne, owned by Associated Radio Co., began broadcasting on the grandly named Brunswick Panatrope.

The first Australian listeners tuned in on crystal wireless sets, in which a "cat's whisker" tickled a lump of crystal to pick up the signal. Records were played on wind-up gramophones, the microphone suspended above the horn. Quartets, quintettes, even choirs squeezed into heavily curtained rooms for a few minutes of glory "on the air". Performers in the studio wore evening dress. After all, you never knew who might be listening.

Programmes started and finished at bewildering times. "News" at 7.36 p.m. was followed by "Boats in call by wireless" at 7.41 p.m. The time itself was a special event. Stations had a love affair with chiming clocks. Big Ben struck the hour on 2FC, while 2BL threw open the window to catch the clock on the GPO. Not to be outdone, 3AR advertised that its 4 p.m. programme item was "GPO Clock says Four". At 5 p.m., it was "GPO Clock says Five", after which the station closed down for an hour's well-earned rest. Mercifully, there were no clocks at all on 6WF Perth.

2BL had reportedly lost £15,000 in its first year and the government decided to change the industry's structure. It established two classes of stations: A-class stations such as 2FC and 2BL (which later became the Australian Broadcasting Commission) were financed by revenue received from licences issued to listeners. B-Class stations received no government support, and had to raise revenue by broadcasting advertisements. To make matters worse, their transmitting signals were limited to 15 miles.

The first 'B-class' licence was issued to C. V. Stephenson whose station 2UE began broadcasting from his Maroubra house on 26 January 1925. It cost Stephenson £750 to build and £9 a week to run. He played the family Pianola rolls and when each roll finished, he rewound it with the microphone open so listeners would know he was still on the air. Then he walked to the cabinet to get a fresh roll, whistling as he went. According to legend, the local butcher rang up to complain one day. "Your horrible whistling is driving me insane. Why don't you tell your listeners the price of my best cuts instead?" The man had a point. Stephenson charged one shilling per announcement.

More stations sprang up, adopting call signs that communicated their ownership, location or agenda. 3DB Melbourne was named after the original licensee, Druleigh Business and Technical College. 2CH was licensed to the Council of Churches, while 2SM stood for St Mark's Presbytery in Drummoyne where the parish priest, Father Meaney, held the licence. 2GB was started by the Theosophical Society, and loftily named in memory of the Italian philosopher Giordino Bruno. Location inspired the names of 2AY Albury, 2BH Broken Hill, and 2KA Katoomba. 2LF Young was actually located at Lambing Flat, while 5KA broadcast from Kintore Avenue, Adelaide.

Soon the glorious amateurs had had their day. Sir Hugh Denison, owner of *The Sun* newspaper, bought 2GB. Sir Keith Murdoch's Melbourne *Herald* bought 3DB in 1929; within six years, Murdoch had interests in eleven of Australia's 65 stations. Other newspapers, originally hostile to the new medium, quietly did the same. Broadcasting had now become a business and being labelled B-class did not help the commercial stations, especially when some of the A-class stations could also broadcast ads. By 1930 they had banded together as the Australian Federation of Commercial Broadcasting Stations and did battle with the Postmaster-General, who controlled the industry. When the ABC was formed in 1932, the Federation President, 2GB's A. E. Bennett, campaigned for equality. Bennett insisted the ABC should leave entertainment to the commercial broadcasters who were more fitted for it. But thanks to licence fees, the ABC had a war chest of £300,000 a year to spend on making programmes.

Bennett was a visionary.

If commercial stations were to have any chance of beating the ABC, he argued, they had to share the cost of making programmes. And it made better business sense for the stations to use transcriptions rather than landlines to cover the vast distances between them. A national broadcast from Sydney would require 4,500 miles of landlines, an expensive proposition, while transcriptions could be despatched by mail for a fraction of the cost. Besides which, the Postmaster-General controlled the landlines and the ABC had first call on them. Not that the PMG landlines were up to broadcasting standard in the first place — it was only possible to get reasonable quality between Sydney and Melbourne. (The PMG had several booster stations between these cities, which effectively took the signal and boosted its strength before passing it to the next station where it was boosted again.)

All of which was reason enough for Bennett to look to America for transcribed programmes. In the process, he would make history when he arrived in Hollywood and encountered the ambitious young Grace Gibson.

DECEMBER 1933. Grace's boss, Freeman Lang, a former Los Angeles radio announcer, called her into his office. He wanted to know what she was doing for the Christmas holidays.

She told him she was going to Big Bear, about a hundred miles from Los Angeles. Everything was planned, she pointed out. It was too late to change it all now.

Lang knew his bright young employee better than she thought. He made her an offer she couldn't refuse.

"There's a man coming in from Australia, from 2GB in Sydney, a Mr. Bennett, to buy some shows," he explained. "I won't be in town because I'm going away on my yacht to Ensenada. But if you meet him and entertain him while he's here, I'll let you have the keys to my car…"

Lang's 16-cylinder Cadillac was a step up from Grace's Ford. Just the thing to be seen driving around Hollywood in. Suddenly, Big Bear could wait. Grace agreed.

When Bennett arrived, Grace swept him up in the Cadillac. He was a short but impressive figure, "a very nice man", she later recalled.

Little did Grace know that Mr. Bennett's favourite movie actress was the serious-faced, lady-like Kay Francis, then at the peak of her career starring in films such as *One Way Passage*, *Trouble in Paradise* and *Cynara*. Innocently he asked about Francis. Had Grace ever met her? *Met her…?* Grace shot him one of her smiles. It just so happened they had *worked in movies together*. (Grace had been Francis's stand-in, riding a horse sidesaddle in the wide shots. In truth, it was the closest Grace ever got to a camera.) With typical chutzpah, Grace made some phone calls. Everything was fixed. The man from 2GB took Kay Francis to dinner.

Bennett was impressed. And more so, in the coming days.

Not only did the 28-year old Grace sell him all the programmes that her company had, but she took him to all the other companies and sold him their programmes too.

It was a whirlwind visit, transcription companies by day, the Hollywood watering holes by night. In Grace's words, "I showed him a good time."

BY ALL accounts Bennett was a man who discovered people. He had given Jack Davey his first break on 2GB, and Grace would arguably be his second major coup.

When he returned to Sydney in 1934, he found he could not only broadcast the transcriptions on 2GB, but also sell them profitably to other stations. But the transcriptions business was new to Australia. Not all stations had suitable turntables. Bennett knew he was onto a winning proposition, but didn't know how to take it forward. His mind turned to Grace Gibson — Kay Francis's good friend Grace.

Bennett cabled Freeman Lang and asked whether he would release Grace for six months to come out to Australia and pioneer the transcription business. He wanted to set up his own transcription company with Grace's help. It would mean more sales for Lang in the long run. Quid pro quo, really.

Lang summoned Grace to his office and they both had a giggle about it.

In common with most Americans in those days, Grace didn't know a thing about Australia. "Which way *is* Australia?" Grace joked. "Down there?"

"I think it'd be a good idea if you went," Lang reassured her. "It'd be a great adventure for you, expenses paid both ways."

So off she went on the first-class liner *Mariposa*.

GRACE stepped ashore in what certainly wasn't Hollywood. Rather, to all intents and purposes, it was still an outpost of the British Empire where sheep outnumbered people, a cultural desert, a conservative, predominantly white Anglo-Saxon society led by a conservative prime minister, Joseph Lyons. History doesn't record Grace's first impressions. Doubtless, she saw the possibility of conquest. Through the eyes of an ambitious young American woman, Sydney must have resembled a large, unsophisticated Midwest city in the States; a city of 1,200,000, isolated at the bottom of the world, deprived of modern ideas, thirsting for the kind of radio entertainment that Grace had packed in her bags. Then again, it was a cut above El Paso! The Harbour Bridge, the world's tallest steel arch bridge, had opened two years earlier and dominated the city's skyline. The bridge expressed the optimism of a young nation, and that would certainly have rubbed off on Grace. Brimming with confidence, she was determined to succeed in her mission.

She discovered a young, brash, swashbuckling radio industry dominated by George Edwards, a fat, failed vaudevillian billed as The Man of a Thousand Voices. He was *everywhere!* In 1934, three of the four top-rating shows — *Inspector Scott of Scotland Yard*, *Treasure Island* and *Peter and Peggy* — were George Edwards's productions. Edwards was really Harold Parks, whose desire to act led him to change his name to Edwards, in honour of the theatrical manager George Edwardes who had befriended him years before in Britain.

Edwards had begun producing and starring in Sunday night dramas in 1932. He played seven or eight different characters in each story, as did his wife Nell Stirling (a chorus line dancer who had also changed her name; she was born Helen Malgrom). Their dramas were broadcast live to air by 2GB, fuelled by scripts dictated to a team of stenographers by the prolific Maurice Francis, and transcribed onto discs for later broadcast in New Zealand. *Inspector Scott* brought Sydney to a standstill for its sponsor Fostars Shoes. A different mystery was presented each week, Monday to Saturday, from 6.58 p.m. to 7.13 p.m. By Saturday, when Inspector Scott finally cornered and denounced the villain, the audience heaved a collective sigh of relief. Presaging *Hawaii Five-O*, Inspector Scott rounded off each weekly drama with the command, "Take him away!"

Edwards played all the male roles; Nell took the female parts. Edwards marked his scripts with different coloured pencils to remind him which voice to use. Having a cast of two made sense: not only did Edwards pocket more profit, the early microphones only worked on one side. But everything George Edwards did was George Edwards's property. Loyalty was negotiable. 2GB was merely his recording facility and the carrier of his programmes.

And that fact had not escaped Bennett. American transcriptions were his insurance policy in the event Edwards folded his tent.

SO, THOUGHT Grace, this is Sydney. Well, Freeman Lang *had* promised her an adventure. Radio was now in her blood, and her instincts served her well.

She decided to stay.

Episode 2

The man from Shanghai

GRACE became the first manager of Bennett's new company — in fact, she even named it — American Radio Transcription Agencies. Its cable address was ARTRANSA. The acronym stuck. When the company recorded its own shows in Sydney, it called itself Artransa. Ironically, it later became one of Grace's major competitors.

She started selling American shows and they sold like wildfire. Lever Bros bought some for national sponsorship. Shows with curious names — *Pinto Pete and His Ranch Boys, Frank Watanabe and the Honorable Archie, Chandu the Magician, Jimmy Allen's Air Adventure* — were all imported by Grace and found willing audiences and sponsors. Saunders the Jewellers, for example, sponsored *Chandu*, played by American Gayne Whitman. Soon *Jimmy Allen* and *Chandu* were rated among the top five most popular Sydney programmes.

Perhaps at last, mused A. E. Bennett, George Edwards had met his match in Grace Gibson.

Artransa was located in Savoy House, 29 Bligh Street, which also housed the Savoy Theatre. The building was the virtual headquarters of Sydney radio.

2GB and 2UE were on the upper floors. So, too, was the Australian Record Company (ARC). A few years later, the Colgate-Palmolive Radio Unit would be based on the sixth floor.

Grace put in place the system for scheduling the programmes and distributing the transcription discs from one station to another across Australia. A newspaper at the time called her "The Highest Paid Woman in Australia". She was earning £40 a week, and, as far as Bennett was concerned, was worth every penny of it.

Radio was becoming big business. A 1934 survey showed that the average listener tuned in for two and a quarter hours each weekday and four hours on weekends. Advertising revenues soared to £1,500,000. By 1935, a quarter-hour programme in Sydney cost its sponsor anywhere from £6 to £13.

In 1936, the axe fell. 2GB had been riding high until Edwards announced his intention to switch to EMI. His unit worked from the HMV studio inside the Columbia record factory at Homebush, whose tall brick chimney was a local landmark for years. The HMV studio was immense; it could swallow the entire Sydney Symphony Orchestra. Edwards used one corner of it. It was like a factory within a factory; cutting 12 to 15 quarter-hour episodes a day was normal. Many were execrable.

Edwards's greatest success came when Byron Wrigley of the chewing gum company got together with Sam Dobbs, the head of Wrigley's advertising agency J. Walter Thompson. Wrigley wanted to sponsor a radio serial, something that would become the Australian equivalent of America's *Amos and Andy*, two white men who delivered their humour and philosophy in African-American voices. Wrigley and Hobbs settled on the characters in Steele Rudd's *On Our Selection*, already a popular film with Bert Bailey as Dad and Peter Finch as a gaunt Dave. They consulted Edwards. Edwards launched *Dad and Dave* on 2UW. He played Dad and most of the menfolk. John Saul, a future Grace Gibson employee, was Dave.

Not only had 2GB lost Edwards; it suddenly found itself fighting Australia's first two commercial radio networks. It was alone, and its fortunes were waning.

AMERICAN radio flourished with the big networks — NBC, ABC, CBS and Mutual. But under Australian regulations, no company could control more than eight stations. If Australia were to have networks, they would have to be organised along cooperative lines, with individual stations sharing centralised programme supply and sales representation.

As it turned out, the advertising agencies and their clients built their own networks.

The Clark Gable movie *The Hucksters* comes to mind. Soap companies and patent medicine makers ruled the airwaves. Radio was a commodity, and the big money, vested in a few hands, dictated its future. Stations were either "in" or "out". Men like George Patterson, Sim Rubensohn and Sam Dobbs in Sydney, and Jack Clemenger in Melbourne, made the shows and called the shots. It was said that Patterson could virtually make or break any radio station by moving programmes in blocks to a competitor. His client, J. V. Moran of Colgate-Palmolive, controlled enough firepower to sponsor more than 20 shows over the years. Meanwhile, J. Walter Thompson worked for Lux, Kelloggs, Wrigleys and Bonnington's Irish Moss cough syrup. Grace got to know them all; Sim Rubensohn, founder of the Hansen-Rubensohn advertising agency (today's McCann-Erickson) especially respected her talent and drive.

The Major Network was a loose collaboration between the stations that got the bulk of the shows and money from the two biggest advertising agencies — 2CH Sydney, 3DB Melbourne, 4BK Brisbane, 5AD Adelaide, 2KO Newcastle and 2GZ Orange, which was regarded as a critical rural component. When 2CH dropped out, 2UE replaced it. Major's agenda was clear enough: programme supply. The second network, the Commonwealth Broadcasting Network, was really only one station — 2UW Sydney — cobbling together interstate affiliates to keep the big sponsors happy.

Major's driving force was the aggressive David Worrall, 3DB's general manager. He had observed the success that Bennett and Grace had enjoyed. And like them, he preferred circulating transcribed programmes to hiring landlines.

When Bennett heard that Worrall planned a Hollywood shopping expedition, he put Grace on the next ship to America.

"You'd better tie these producers up because nobody else from Australia has ever approached them before," he told her. This trip, she had to get them all to sign exclusive contracts with 2GB.

So Grace boarded the *Mariposa*, where she conspired to sit at the table of a very nice ship's officer.

GRACE returned in 1938 with 62 new productions — 3,412 transcription discs in all, including 130 episodes of *Charlie Chan*, "starring Cy Kendall and an all-star Hollywood cast". Two of the shows were musical: *Dream Time*, a programme of songs, poems and organ music "in meditative mood", and *Swamp Caesar*, melodies of the sunny South and Negro spirituals "such as only the coloured people of the southern part of the States can sing". Another show was a precursor of the programmes Grace herself would make 30 years later: a series of 100 five-minute short features called *Lucky Victims of Misfortune*, 100 five-minute short features "dramatising incidents that come under this classification".

Now Grace and Bennett could boast that 2GB and Artransa represented the cream of Hollywood radio. These long-forgotten names were the formidable studios in their day: American Radio Features Syndicate, Bowman Deute Cummings, Earnshaw-Young, Electro-Vox, Famar Recording System, Freeman Lang, Hollywood Radio Attractions, R. U. McIntosh & Associates, Radio Programmes Syndicate, Radio Transcription Company of America, Radio Release Inc, Standard Radio Advertising Company, Titan Productions, Universal Transcription Company and World Broadcasting System, Inc.

They had beaten Worrall to the mark, and 2GB's publicity material confidently crowed:

It would be foolish not to admit that the immense popularity that 2GB achieved during 1934 was largely built up on the merits of Electrical Transcriptions, and that that popularity radiated to the firms who were wise in sponsoring these transcriptions when, as far as Australia was concerned, they were still in the nature of an experiment. At the time, it might have seemed that their popularity was largely due to their novelty, but now that their period of probation is over, it can be seen that they supplied an ever-growing need for variety in Australian broadcasting … In sponsoring electrical transcriptions, the advertiser gives the listener good entertainment, entertainment that already bears an international hall-mark … Transcriptions have won themselves an unassailable place on 2GB's programmes. The public wants them, and is grateful to the sponsor who gives it the opportunity of hearing them. Thus the sponsor makes a friend of the public, in a way unprecedented in advertising, and he puts the public in the right mood to buy his goods. What more can the public, the sponsor or the station ask?

FOR years, 2GB had stood alone. Now, buoyed by its guaranteed supply of American programmes, it rallied its friends and formed a network of its own.

On 1 July 1938 Macquarie Broadcasting Services Pty Ltd registered the name Macquarie Network. Financed by the Denison family, owners of 2GB, it represented the best capital city stations excluded from the Major network: 2GB Sydney, 2CA Canberra, 3AW Melbourne, 4BH Brisbane, 5DN Adelaide, 6IX Perth and 7HO Hobart. Another 39 cooperating stations fell into line behind them. Jack Ridley's 2GZ Orange resisted the new network's overtures and stayed with Major; 2BS Bathurst and 2DU Dubbo happily took its place.

Freddie Daniel, a relation of the Denisons, suggested the name "Macquarie". Governor Macquarie had been "the builder of the nation", somebody who got things done. Inspired by the NBC Network in America, Daniel urged the family to support the idea. In keeping with

Australian regulations, the network did not own the stations; member stations held shares in the network, which acted as their sales agent. Production was centralised in Sydney and Melbourne.

The first programme produced by Macquarie was *Doctor Mac*, sponsored by DeWitts Pills. Veteran actor Lou Vernon began each episode with the words, "Aye, it's me, Doctor Mac…" The second Macquarie production, based on a popular American show, was *The Quiz Kids* compered by the portly John Dease and sponsored by Johnson & Johnson. From such humble beginnings Macquarie would eventually become the largest producer of variety, quiz and drama programmes in the British Commonwealth. By the time war broke out in 1939, Macquarie had made stars of Lou Vernon, Dick Bentley and Jack Davey. At last, individual radio stations had found a way to control their own destinies, and give the ABC a run for its money as well.

Grace, meanwhile, burned the candle at both ends. She loved nothing more than a good party, but now her hectic social life had a new imperative — wartime charity work — and with it came friendships with newspaper baron Frank Packer, owner of the *Daily Telegraph* and *Women's Weekly*, and socialite Nola Dekyvere.

By that time, Grace had been seven years in Australia. She had no plans to leave or live elsewhere. The fact that her career might soon be in turmoil never occurred to her. Not only was the war getting closer to home, the second man who would transform her life was on the horizon.

IT WAS 1941, and Grace was selling fundraising tickets at one of Nola Dekyvere's Red Cross charity balls. She heard an unfamiliar voice, looked up, and there was the dashing Randell Robert Ronald M'Donell Parr. Everyone called him Ronnie.

Ronnie was the compleat Mills & Boon hero — Ronald Colman and David Niven in one; handsome, tall, athletic, and armed with a seductive

British persona that a girl from El Paso found impossible to resist. He was two or three years older than Grace, down from Shanghai to join the Australian forces because he admired their fighting record.

In Hollywood jargon, Ronnie's "backstory" might well have been penned at MGM. Born in Tibet of Irish parents, Ronnie could trace his ancestry all the way back to Catherine Parr. His father had been in the Royal Irish Fusiliers and served as a British customs agent in Tibet. His mother was a southern Irish belle. Ronnie was the product of an English public school, where he had sufficiently polished his skills as a boxer to become a British Empire amateur boxing champion. (If you looked at him closely, he had cauliflower ears.) His polo-playing ability was equally impressive. King George VI's brother, the Duke of Kent, had been a frequent partner; George of Kent died in 1942 when his RAF Sunderland, bound for Iceland, crashed in bad weather.

Ronnie had served in the Black Watch. One day Ronnie and his compatriots posed for a photograph. They had been swimming naked, wearing only their sporrans. Just as the camera clicked, Ronnie lifted his.

Like many another scion of an impoverished upper class family, the young Ronnie had been despatched to Shanghai to seek his, and hopefully, his family's fortune. He had worked as a salesman for Shell, sold insurance, and joined the Far Eastern Service. As was customary, young gentlemen such as Ronnie were called upon to entertain the daughters of the British colonial elite. Correct etiquette was observed unfailingly. The British roses were always returned to their homes with absolute decorum, after which Ronnie and the lads ventured out to the fleshpots of Shanghai.

He *was* the perfect gentleman, but definitely no prude, just the fellow to tame Grace.

Their attraction was immediate. But no sooner had they fallen in love than they were separated. Ronnie was sent to the Middle East and New Guinea. Grace left for America to buy more programmes.

For once, her timing left a lot to be desired.

The *Mariposa* sailed from Honolulu on 6 December, the day before the Japanese attacked the naval base at Pearl Harbour. By the time she reached America, war was raging across the Pacific. Grace was stranded, with no idea when or how she could return to Sydney. "They had more important things to put on ships than single women," she complained.

It was back to square one — the Hollywood transcription business.

Grace's lucky stars did not desert her. The legendary "Cash-and-Carry" Pyle, president of the Radio Transcription Company of America, had died suddenly. Grace, something of a legend herself, was offered the post of managing director. From being an errand girl and saleswoman, she now presided over the golden years of Hollywood radio. As she would later recount, "That was when I really learned the radio transcriptions business."

In her bags had been an Artransa show, *Doctors Courageous*. By the time she eventually left America, she had the programme playing on 250 American radio stations.

MEANWHILE back in Sydney, things were changing on the home front. Newsprint restrictions were driving thousands of advertisers on to radio. And with a single stroke of the pen, a wartime Australian government, eager to save currency, banned the importation of American transcriptions. Not only was the radio industry booming; overnight it had to stand on its own feet and have a totally Australian voice.

New names sprang up, feeding radio's insatiable appetite. The old guard — Artransa and EMI's George Edwards — found themselves competing with British Australian Programmes (BAP), Amalgamated Wireless Australasia (AWA), 2UW's Fidelity, and 2UE's Paul Jacklin. Macquarie beefed up production, and opened its Phillip Street auditorium in 1942. That same year, 2UW opened its radio theatre in George Street near Gowings; hailed as "The Theatre Beautiful", it boasted "every modern principle of acoustical science and an atmosphere of complete intimacy in theatre planning". Soon, it was packing in 120,000 people every year. In Melbourne, John Hickling and Hector Crawford entered the fray.

IN 1944 Ronnie cabled Grace: "Sorry you won't be in Sydney because I have three months' leave."

Grace pulled strings. A call to her old Red Cross pal Frank Packer got her onto a Swedish cargo ship. She arrived in Sydney a week before Ronnie. Despite wartime secrecy, she discovered that he would be arriving via Townsville. She hurried north and called on the manager of the local radio station, 4TO, who pulled strings of his own and traced Ronnie's movements.

When Ronnie's troop train pulled into Townsville, Grace was waiting on the platform. They spent the night in a railway carriage before returning to Sydney.

The following week everything happened.

With Frank Packer as best man, Grace married Warrant-Officer Ronnie Parr at the Registrar-General's office followed by a reception at the Blue Room of Usher's Hotel. That same week, she hung out her shingle. Grace Gibson Radio Productions was in business.

Episode 3
"A Grace Gibson Radio Production"

GRACE'S decision to go it alone met with more than wartime scepticism. The established networks and production houses, with their entrenched sponsors and affiliations, did not exactly welcome competition — especially from someone who knew the business as well as Grace Gibson. "You have no idea what Artransa and EMI and every one of the producers tried to do to me," Grace would recall. "I could feel the stilettoes going into my back from the men."

Nobody expected her to succeed.

One broadcasting executive swore, "We'll break you."

Grace replied, "Well, you'd better have a very big gun because I'm coming after you with a cannon."

Within six months, Grace had five national radio programmes up and running. Her first shows, *Here Are the Facts* and *Drama of Medicine*, also sold well overseas.

So much for the doomsayers.

GRACE was still under contract to 2GB when she returned to Australia in 1944. Her old mentor A. E. Bennett had long since gone. She broke her contract with 2GB quite deliberately and walked out. Macquarie tried to stop her. "They said the scripts I was using were theirs when they hadn't even paid me for them." They threatened to sue her and she said, "Do it." Twelve months would pass before 2GB broadcast its first Grace Gibson show, *Mr & Mrs North*, on 20 September 1945. As far as that station was concerned, Grace was a latter-day George Edwards. They'd brought her to Australia, given her her big break, and now she was double-crossing them. She was a mercenary, and not to be trusted. Not that everyone shared that view; Percy Campbell, production manager of Macquarie, had attended her wedding: "She was magnificent, a brilliant programme lady and a mighty good business lady, and that was Grace. We became great friends over the years, and I bought a lot of her programmes for the Macquarie network. When she departed we remained wonderful friends, we saw a lot of each other, until the day she passed on."

Rumours abounded.

There was speculation that she was still in cahoots with American transcription companies. In truth, if Grace wanted American scripts, she had to buy them at market prices just like anyone else. She certainly had her Hollywood contacts, and her experience, and she still knew her way round the American industry, but that was where the matter ended.

Another malicious rumour was that Grace had a secret hoard of US dollars. Her friends knew otherwise. She was actually "without a cracker" and "on the breadline"; in fact, she probably had no more than £500 to roll. "Ronnie didn't marry me for my money," she was fond of telling friends. She was so undercapitalised that she was never certain where the rent was coming from. Grace personally packed and despatched her first discs from an airline office in Phillip Street. "I sold 'em, so I packed 'em!" she chuckled years later.

Her accountant had told her, "When the money starts coming, it's going to come in big chunks." And Grace recalled his prediction: "It did, but gee, it was a *long* while coming…" Grace was always proud of her success. "I proved it wasn't necessarily a man's world. It was *very* satisfying…"

RADIO production was peaking. Everything had to be recorded in Australia. Imported shows would not be allowed on air again until the early 1950s.

Grace had an impressive cast of competitors.

In Sydney, AWA, EMI, Ron R. Beck, 2UE, Associated Programmes, the Australian Record Company (which today is Sony Music Entertainment), British Australian Programmes, Hepworth Productions, and 2UW's Fidelity Radio all churned out serials. Macquarie produced programmes for its top-rating network, as did its sister company Artransa; Artransa, though, could sell shows to anyone.

In Melbourne, pre-war transcription companies like Featuradio, Legionnaire and Televox had merged into Broadcast Exchange of Australia (BEA), managed by Hector Crawford until he left and opened his own production company in 1945. Thanks to the swift technical expertise of BEA's legendary engineer Monty Maizels, epic serials flowed from its studios at 32 Market Street: *Delia of Four Winds, The Markhams, His Heritage, Simon Masterton* and *Lavender Grove*.

The young Morris West started Australasian Radio Productions (ARP) in 1945 in a hessian-lined studio over a Smith Street, Collingwood pharmacy. Five years earlier, West had left the Christian Brothers before taking his final vows. His biggest show was *The Burtons of Banner Street*. Its sponsor, Bex, insisted on approving all the scripts of its 2,000 episodes in advance; sex, politics, religion and liquor were out. West produced 40 quarter-hours a week, including *Reach For the Sky, On the Beach, Chequerboard*, and *They're a Weird Mob*, the only commercially produced serial ever sold to the ABC. West left to write novels. In the mid-1950s the company's name changed to Australasian Radio and Television Productions (ART) and made TV commercials.

Former advertising executive John Hickling recorded 20 episodes a day in his studio, often writing them himself and operating his own panel. At the opposite end of the spectrum, Donovan Joyce became famous for strongly plotted dramas and meticulous production. His serials included *Office Wife* and *The Devil's Duchess*. Such was his reputation that in the 1950s, the Major Network advanced him £75,000 to develop new programmes.

The stakes were getting higher.

Radio shows were building famous brands. Y-Cough sponsored *Yes, What?* Bonnington's Irish Moss sponsored *Mrs 'Obbs*. Kelloggs owned *Martins Corner* and *Smoky Dawson*. And Stamina self-supporting trousers broadcast dramatisations of the lives of *Men of Stamina*.

The question was, would there be room for yet another radio production house?

TYPICAL of Grace, she set up her company at Savoy House in Bligh Street, right under the noses of 2UE and the Australian Record Company.

Her good friend Frank Packer wanted to back her, but in Grace's words, "I didn't care for that because he wanted 51% of the company". Instead, another powerful friend stepped up to the plate.

Sim Rubensohn provided an interest-free financial agreement and set about obtaining sponsors to protect his investment. Rubensohn, who propagated camellias in his spare time, was Grace's "angel", no strings attached.

Grace rented two offices, roughly the size of two large suburban lounge rooms, facing each other across a dingy, black-and-white tiled corridor. Savoy House, for all its strategic importance, was a stuffy building with no air conditioning. The windows looked out onto bleak air wells, and the New South Wales Club next door. When the film *Fantasia* was playing at the Savoy Theatre downstairs, the sound leaked up from the cinema into Grace's office. The staff could tell the time by the changing sequences of the film. The Sorcerer's Apprentice theme, amplified by the cinema's speakers, was particularly intrusive.

The staff shared one office. Betty Gondolf was Grace's secretary; she also meticulously cut stencils for the scripts and booked the casts for recording. Loris Gunn, the full-time script typist, shared a desk with Betty Barnard, a part-timer and an old friend of Grace's who would later become manager. Director-writer-actor-narrator Reg Johnston worked from a third desk. Transcription discs were stored in a wooden cabinet along one wall, facing a cluttered worktable where discs were packed and a hand-operated Roneo machine printed out scripts.

Grace's office was across the hall. It was exactly the same size, but with a better carpet. Grace had a penchant for green ink. Two fountain pens had pride of place on her desk, alongside a little snowman in a round glass ball. When it was turned upside down, the snow fell. Every Monday morning fresh flowers were brought in from a florist in Hunter Street.

Grace often entertained station managers over a chicken or ham salad lunch sent up from the Green Parrot restaurant in the basement next door, while she previewed her shows on a large playback unit. Invariably she talked all the way through a programme, in case they didn't like it.

Bottles of Scotch, gin and brandy were stashed in the drawer of her filing cabinet. On Friday afternoon, with a lookout posted in the corridor, the staff went in and helped themselves to a much-needed drink.

There was no money to build her own recording studio. Instead, she hired the Australian Recording Company studio in the same building — preferably the bigger "A" studio. The bills came in weekly, and credit terms extended for a whole seven days.

BETTY Gondolf was no stranger to Savoy House. She had started in radio with 2GB as producer E. Mason Wood's secretary. The first radio script she typed was *Doctor Mac*. She had no sooner settled into life at 2GB than the Colgate-Palmolive Radio Unit was formed. It, too, was based in Savoy House and produced Jack Davey's *Calling the Stars*, *The Youth Show* and *Rise and Shine* for the Army. As *The Youth Show* secretary, Gondolf found herself surrounded by stars. All the artists were under 21 and she was their age.

"I really wasn't paid by 2GB very long. I became secretary to *The Youth Show* producer, Russell Scott, and then Mark Makeham. Jack Davey was in the next office. We didn't work together because we were on different shows, but we used to wave to each other."

The Youth Show combined music, comedy and drama. Under Makeham's tutelage, many talented young Australians had their first taste of fame. Teenage oboist Charles Mackerras and young jazz clarinetist Don Burrows were regulars. So was singer-comedienne Joy Nichols, later a BBC radio star in *Take it from Here*. Young performers Bill Kerr, Colin Croft, Margo Lee, Lloyd Berrell and Bettie Dickson became household names.

They were heady days for the young secretary. "We used to have 2,000 people at the Trocadero every Tuesday night. If I went over the road after rehearsal to have a grilled sausage sandwich with Bettie Dickson, we couldn't get back through the doors again. I never walked in till all the lights were right down because I was most embarrassed. I'd walk round very slowly and sit down next to Mark Makeham at the front with my notebook. Even though it was radio we had all these lovely girls come out, all dressed in beautiful clothes, because of the audience. Every comedy actor was dressed up. It was very popular. They were the most wonderful working days I could ever imagine having."

George Patterson Advertising ran the Colgate-Palmolive unit. "George Patterson often came into our office. He was a very nice man, quite elderly then, walking with a stick. He was very easy to talk to, and you would never have known that he owned a huge advertising agency. He was very interested in the artists in *The Youth Show*." Lionel Shave from the agency was another good friend.

But when compere Robin Ordell joined the Air Force, and Colin Croft went into the Army, Gondolf thought she should "go and do my bit." She spent three and a half years in the Air Force. "When I came out I thought, what am I going to do with myself? Radio's too hectic, I thought. I was walking down a street and I bumped into Betty Barnard who was working with Grace Gibson. Betty asked me if I'd like a job with Grace. She told me to go up and see her, and I got the job."

Gondolf's first encounter with Grace was intimidating. "She was a tall woman, very overbearing I could say, and she almost frightened me. I knew she'd be strict. I typed scripts, did the filing and the accounts. We had some very good writers. I couldn't wait to read their scripts, that's how good the shows were." But not all the writers delivered their work on time. Michael Plant and Lindsay Hardy were notable offenders. It was really panic stations with Lindsay Hardy; when he'd finally finished a page, she'd snatch it from his typewriter and put it straight on to the stencil.

Gondolf also helped book the casts. "In those days, not many artists were with agencies. I'd have to ring their number all day to catch them when they came home. Some were out all day. I might have got five of the cast finally booked, but then the sixth person would say, 'Oh, Betty darling, I'm sorry, I'm at the ABC all that day.' I'd burst out crying and start all over again. It took a lot out of you." Peter Finch was notoriously hard to contact, but she got on well with Michael Pate. "We were good friends."

In those days, Gondolf worked every third Saturday and received two weeks' holiday a year. "Every year Grace used to give us a day out. One year we went to Palm Beach. But I never felt really close to her. I never felt as though she was a really true friend. I just felt she was my boss, and I worked hard and earned my money, and that was about it. Her great aim in life was to pay more income tax than any of her socialite friends. She was very proud of that. She was a great socialite, a great friend of Nola

Dekyvere." Grace, said Gondolf, was a very determined lady. "But she had the most beautiful husband."

When Grace made a visit to the States, Gondolf was left in charge. "I had the whole place to look after. I lost a stone in weight. I didn't have to do actual sales, but the fellow she had drank a lot and I really had the most terrible experience because of that. But Reg Johnston who was producing at that time was a tower of strength. Without him to back me up I don't know how I could have coped. I was just so glad to see her come back."

But there were compensations: a young panel operator at the Australian Record Company on the third floor. John Woodward was very good at fixing broken radios, and Betty Gondolf's broke down regularly.

JOHN Woodward first met Grace when she was a client. He had joined AWA as a beam wireless operator in 1936. At that time AWA operated marine and coastal wireless services, manufactured domestic radios, and produced radio programmes. Three years later, Woodward had progressed to the recording department on £1 a week. "In those post-Depression days that was good money. I used to get a penny a week pocket money." After another two years, Woodward went to sea as a radio officer in the merchant navy, but was called back into recording. He worked all day in the AWA studios, and at night broadcast for the US Army to the underground movement in the Philippines.

AWA's main drama studio was located at 72 Clarence Street, directly behind the iconic AWA Building in York Street. Edward Howell was in charge of production for AWA, and the studio also accepted outside work. One such client was John Hickling, who once came up from Melbourne and recorded a 52-episode show in five days. Woodward recorded the Lux Radio Theatre, directed by the glamorous Harry Dearth. "If you talked to Harry in the office, you couldn't understand him. He spoke so fast. But on the air he was crystal clear." In 1945 Woodward recorded the first episodes of AWA's marathon serial *When a Girl Marries*, "dedicated to those who are in love, and to all those who can remember".

In this digital recording age, Woodward's technical equipment sounds prehistoric. "The AWA recording machines were run by electric power. The programmes were recorded onto metal-based masters, coated with lacquer, which could be recoated for the next recording. At EMI, however, the machines were powered by gravity feed. Imagine a giant cuckoo clock. Large weights had to be hauled to the required height to provide enough power for the duration of the recording." EMI cut its shows onto wax masters, large circular slabs of wax about two inches thick that were "shaved" for the next recording.

Grace's first show, *Here Are the Facts*, was recorded at AWA. Woodward was the panel operator. "I'll always remember her coming in with a black astrakhan coat and black hat. She was a very domineering person. She knew what she wanted. And if she didn't get it, boy oh boy…" It was one of the few occasions that Grace attended a recording.

Woodward also recorded a lot of work for Lionel Shave at George Patterson. It was Shave who persuaded him to move across to the Australian Record Company. As ARC's senior panel operator, Woodward was then involved in all of Grace's recording work, as well as spillover work on *Doctor Mac* for 2GB.

By a happy coincidence, his future wife typed many of Grace's scripts, the same girl from downstairs whose radio was always breaking down.

GRACE knew her limitations. She did not sit in the control room and direct the performances. "There are people who can write and act," she said. "I can sell." As a friend wryly observed: "She was smart in ways we never even dreamed of. She never did anything she couldn't do."

Actor Michael Pate starred in many of her first productions. "Grace never came to the studio except to say, 'Hello everybody, how are you this morning?' or to inquire about somebody, or to congratulate somebody. But she didn't want to waste one minute of time. Don't let it be said that Grace Gibson wasted Grace Gibson's money…"

Grace was the showman, the entrepreneur. She gathered a loyal staff around her; some of them would still be employees when she retired in 1978. She certainly had her opinions and shaped her productions with infinite care. She focused on the scripts first. But was her contribution simply that of editor, critic, and den mother, or did she exercise her own brand of creativity?

In the view of one Gibson cast member: "I didn't think she was even vaguely creative at any stage, that was the last thing I would have said. She was just a tough businesswoman and she managed to keep about her some very clever people."

If nothing else, Grace's years in Hollywood had taught her the value of nurturing creative relationships. And the first clever person she engaged was Lynn Foster.

Foster was an inspired choice: a freelance writer-director with a proven track record in radio drama, and the first woman to have directed a national radio serial, *Big Sister*. She was a disciplined professional who shared Grace's ideals. Both women demanded perfection from casts and colleagues. They were soul mates, and each had something to prove. (In 1949 Foster left for England where she wrote radio and TV scripts for the BBC. She returned to Australia in the 1960s and was writer and script editor on such top-rating television shows as *Mavis Bramston* and the controversial serial, *Number 96*.)

The first four audition discs they cut were sold nationally.

Foster wrote Grace's first show, *Here Are The Facts*. Ron Randell was the compere. It premiered on 2CH.

Sim Rubensohn's client Sterling Pharmaceutical bought Grace's second show, *Drama of Medicine*, and ran it nationally in both Australia and New Zealand. These dramatised self-contained quarter-hour stories of heroic doctors and nurses, and significant medical discoveries, proved to be one of Grace's most successful shows. It was sold throughout the world and eventually in America. Foster wrote the first scripts and other Australian writers carried on for a total of 768 episodes over 15 years.

Another Hansen-Rubensohn client bought her third show — a series of self-contained half-hour plays bannered *Nyal Radio Playhouse*, Nyal being an acronym for The New York and London Pharmaceutical Company. Again, Foster directed. Rubensohn must have been determined to recoup his investment: *Drama of Medicine* and *Nyal Radio Playhouse* ran on both 2UE and 2CH simultaneously.

Grace's fourth show, *Mr and Mrs North*, went to air in September 1945. Another pharmaceutical company sponsored it nationally — the Knox Drug Company, through McClelland Advertising, for a product called Cystex. Veteran actress Fifi Banvard directed.

Hollywood Holiday, Grace's first daytime serial, was sold to J. Walter Thompson and aired on 2UW. Bill Moloney, one of Sydney's most prolific writers, scripted the show.

"Grace was very lucky," said a longtime associate. "She had people around her who helped develop her organisation and got it going, because she knew it was going to be difficult."

Disgruntled local writers created some of those difficulties. They accused Grace of buying cheap American scripts to the detriment of Australian talent. Grace, they said, was cutting corners in order to start her business. They could not have been more wrong. Grace had very little money to outlay on anything, least of all Hollywood scripts. Only three of her first 12 shows were produced from American scripts: *Nyal Radio Playhouse, Mr and Mrs North*, and *The Shadow*. The rest were all written by Australians: *Here Are The Facts, Drama of Medicine, Hollywood Holiday, Story of Flight, Romances of Famous Jewels, Australian Story, Out of the Night, Till the End of Time,* and *The Bishop's Mantle*.

GRACE was in business for the long haul. She had an eye fixed on the future. Actors and actresses assigned the rights in their performances in perpetuity to Grace's company. It was the same for scriptwriters; they assigned all copyrights in their work to Grace Gibson Radio Productions in writing. If you wrote it or spoke it, Grace owned it.

She also knew the value of publicity. Every show she recorded ended with the words: "A Grace Gibson Radio Production". Soon that phrase would be firmly embedded in Australia's national consciousness.

Episode 4

Golden age, Midas touch

AUSTRALIA shrugged off the war years. A decade of optimism had dawned. But Sydney was still a far cry from Hollywood. Steam trains chugged around the suburbs. Trams clattered over the Harbour Bridge. Sydney's West was covered with chicken farms, market gardens, orchards and scrub.

All manner of vendors and tradesmen paraded through the suburban streets: the milk-o, the bottle-o, the rabbito, the garbo. Men sold oysters in bottles and long, wooden poles that propped up washing lines. (The Hills Hoist was still in the future.) Local bakeries delivered bread in horse-drawn carts. Icemen replenished ice chests. The san-o carried away the night soil in a truck with dozens of evil-smelling compartments.

In the city proper, someone wrote "Eternity" on the footpaths. Others scrawled "Vote No" on railway embankments. The eccentric Bea Miles in raincoat and eyeshade hijacked unwary taxi drivers and recited poetry, refusing to leave their cabs.

Everyone preferred formality. Even friends and neighbours addressed each other as "Mr" or "Mrs". The wife was still "the good woman", her place was in the home, and her weekly treat was community singing at the local cinema, shelling peas while she warbled *Daisy, Daisy* or *Mocking Bird Hill*. She went visiting for afternoon tea in a large hat and a rather shabby coat. Every suburban main street had grocers with names like Moran & Cato or Broadhead & Barcham, where men in white coats deftly measured out tea, biscuits and sugar into paper bags. A milliner, a haberdasher, at least two or three cake shops, possibly two or more cinemas were common. Priests wore black. Nuns wore habits. Every week men trooped into the local Masonic Hall carrying small, mysterious cases. The *Bulletin* was published under a masthead that proclaimed "Australia for the white man". On hot summer nights, people "took the air" by walking around the block. Very few had a car, let alone a telephone. The streets were uncrowded. As time progressed, sturdy British Austins and Vauxhalls found they were sharing the road with the first Holdens.

Glamour in Sydney was afternoon tea at Farmers department store serenaded by ladies playing violins, or a visit to the Prince Edward Theatre where the organ rose majestically from the pit.

Throughout this "age of innocence", wireless was the common thread. It was arguably more real, more palpable, more glamorous than television ever was. Radio mattered. People booked tickets months in advance for the Macquarie Auditorium in Phillip Street to see Jack Davey or a play. 2CH's tower atop the AWA Building in York Street dominated the skyline. Like radio itself, the tower was a landmark in the life of the city.

Saturday night at the local flicks was a treat. For the rest of the week, the wireless was Hollywood.

The voices Australians listened to became an indelible part of their lives. They put faces to the voices in their minds, and fingers to their lips as whole families sat around huge radiograms or listened to Bakelite mantel radios in the lounge room. Incredible characters with bizarre names peopled the minds of listeners: the Fairy Godmother, the Sky Pilot, the Jungle Doctor, Jason and the Argonauts. In every school playground, children reenacted the shows they had heard the night before while they drank their free government-supplied milk. Radio advertising was folksy; one famous commercial promised that "the steady sip,

sip, sip of Bonnington's Irish Moss, made out of a rare seaweed found only on the north coast of Ireland" would spell relief for colds and flu. Meanwhile, Aeroplane Jelly proclaimed "the quality's high as the name will imply…"

Radio steadily developed its own conventions.

Through all those golden years, serials for housewives were broadcast four mornings a week, Monday to Thursday. Friday was shopping day, and no one was home. Until American-style shopping centres mushroomed in the suburbs, housewives went into "town" (the CBD) to do their important shopping. Thus, common sense dictated that radio serials should always be divisible by four: 104 quarter-hour episodes could be played four a week, Monday to Thursday, for 26 weeks; 208 episodes could be played four a week and run the full year.

Friday morning drama addicts had to content themselves with self-contained quarter-hour or half-hour stories that broke up the shopping guides and community singing. (And on Friday nights, when Australians trooped off to the movies, even Jack Davey and Bob Dyer took a break; at least three city stations concentrated on sport and previews of the Saturday racing.)

As time went by, a distinct daily listening pattern emerged.

The breakfast session appealed to a constantly changing audience of men, women and children, with popular music, frequent time calls, news and weather reports, designed to see people off to work or school. By 9 a.m., the household bustle had subsided. The mid-morning programmes were dedicated to the housewife, providing her with dramatic serials, music and specialised service programmes. And every weekday morning, virtually every radio station in Australia broadcast the announcement: "The time is ten o'clock and the Commonwealth Bank is now open for business."

With lunch, the tempo increased. The midday news was followed by bright music; the afternoon audience was similar to the morning, but fewer serials were heard. Stations concentrated on music, competitions and requests. When serials were played, they were more dramatic than their morning counterparts.

By late afternoon children were coming home from school, intent on teen-time sessions like 2UE's *Rumpus Room*, shows like the ABC's *Argonauts Club*, and serials like *Superman*, *Tarzan*, and *The Air Adventures of Biggles*.

Early evening shows were aimed at a family audience. *Martin's Corner* and *When a Girl Marries* were tasked with building and holding the numbers; once eight o'clock came, things got really serious. The more expensive programmes, paid for by the big sponsors — plays, comedies, variety and quiz shows — played to peak audiences until 9.30 p.m. Even as transmission wound down for the day, every effort was made to hold listeners so they would leave the dial set on the station for breakfast in the morning. (Only a handful of stations in Australia, such as 2UW, broadcast 24 hours a day.)

Sunday was the big night at home. *The Lux Radio Theatre*, the *Macquarie Theatre* and the *Caltex Theatre* were performed "live" to vast national audiences. (Nothing has changed. Even today, television channels premiere their biggest-rating shows on Sunday nights.)

This was radio's Golden Age, and Grace was the girl with the Midas touch.

REG Johnston was Grace's first production manager. He had left North Sydney Boys' High School at 17, and walked in off the street to ask about a job at 2GB. He was hired on the spot. From cadet announcer he graduated to scriptwriting, producing and compering Macquarie Network shows. Advertising agency J. Walter Thompson hired him to do all the commercial announcing for Lux and the *Amateur Hour*, working with Dick Fair. Next came a year as assistant producer to Paul Jacklin, programme manager at 2UE, followed by freelancing as a writer, narrator and producer for the ABC.

True to form, Grace knew talent when she saw it. She hired Johnston to direct *Hollywood Holiday* and adapt American scripts for *Mr & Mrs North*. Thus began one of radio's greatest partnerships.

Australian actor Alan White, today resident in London, first met Johnston when he was directing children's shows for 2GB together with his wife, Judy Young. "They popularised the easygoing 'chat style' show, *Here and there with Judy and Reg*, for the daily kids' hour." Johnston also produced and directed serials. White was in *The Last of the Mohicans*, and shows like *Dumbo* and *Pinocchio* for the Friday Night *Disney Hours* presented from the Macquarie Auditorium. "Reg narrated them and played many parts himself."

When White returned to civilian life after the war, Johnston was Grace's right-hand man and the artistic soul of the company. "Their shows were respected by the whole profession and the audience ratings were the highest. Reg and Grace were peas in a pod in their tastes and enthusiasm. They were both workaholics. I can never remember them disagreeing." By 1947 Reg was directing *Out of the Night, The Shadow, Caltex Star Theatre, Till the End of Time, Tales of the Supernatural,* and *Drama of Medicine*.

White attributed much of Johnston's success to his perfect sense of radio timing. "*Night Beat's* tuneable tom-tom opening is an example." His theatrical productions were equally remarkable, White recalls. "I was in Giradoux's *Amphitryon 38* at the independent theatre in 1950, with Dinah Shearing, Michael Pate and Margo Lee, which was a huge success — it literally drew the town and was a sell-out."

Actors venerated Johnston. It was a privilege when he cast you. And you gave him your best, without fail.

Michael Pate was recording a show for Johnston one day, and instead of saying "drowned" said "drownded". It was an unforgivable sin. "Why in God's name would I say 'he drownded himself'? You can't help it;

these things do pop out occasionally. I was horrified and I said, 'Oh Reg, I'm *terribly* sorry…' We all did things like that. Those things happened." Pate believed that Johnston had "a nice fluidness" to his direction. After a rehearsal, Johnston went into the studio and discussed each actor's role and interpretation. "He didn't interfere too much. He wouldn't give you a reading of what he wanted before the recording."

It was a different story for his casting girl. Johnston would tell her the actors he wanted for the three leading characters of a half-hour play. If he didn't get them he would say, "Go to buggery, I won't do it, get another script." He rarely if ever compromised. Once he wanted Peter Finch for a half-hour play called *If I Were King*. Finch was going away and not in the mood to answer his phone. Johnston had no hesitation in casting Leonard Teale instead. Many years later, a radio interviewer innocently told Teale how he had once been the obvious replacement for Peter Finch. Teale was not amused.

Nor was Grace amused by the fact that Johnston travelled to and from his Mosman home by ferry. She always complained about him taking home a briefcase bulging with precious scripts. "What if the ferry sank?" she grumbled.

Being Johnston's panel operator brought Woodward more than the occasional challenge. "He pretty well drove me up the wall with his search for perfection, but he achieved it." Woodward recalled the extremes he went to in creating the most realistic sound effects. "Sound effects were limited. I had two hundred 10-inch discs from the Standard library, so we had to improvise in the studio."

Recorded sound effects played by the panel operator were marked on the script as "C.O." If the effects had to be created in the studio, they were marked "STUDIO". The studio contained a baffling array of sound effects apparatus: a large box with different doors and locks, gravel trays, and three or four different timber surfaces for actors to walk on, and a lot of fruit and vegetables.

"The auditors at ARC used to look at me sideways and say, there's an expense chit here for cabbages. If we'd been doing *The Shadow*, and somebody was knifed, you stuck a knife in a cabbage. When a body fell down, we threw a mango or a paw-paw onto a slab of marble." Actor Redmond Phillips once brought a very big paw-paw for the sound of a head being squashed. It was all grist for Woodward's mill. Years later, when Dr Paul's wife Virginia gave birth to a baby, Woodward rushed home to record his own daughter Jan, then three months old, but first locking an anxious mother out of the room while he prompted the child to deliver a wide range of sounds.

Johnston not only inspired his writers and casts. He was good copy for the newspapers. Readers, it seemed, devoured every word they could about radio. Any chance to go behind the scenes into Sydney's own homegrown Hollywood was not to be missed:

> Seated in the studio control-room, I could watch the panel operator working at his instrument panel, and look through the glass wall at the actors in the studio.
>
> Producer Reg Johnston, armed with scripts, blue pencil, and stopwatch (the latter essential to achieve the split-second timing needed to record each episode), also took his seat in the control room, and sharp on the hour the first rehearsal began.
>
> The actors' voices came through to us over a two-way amplifier. The producer can speak back to the studio by merely flicking down a switch.
>
> The first rehearsal was an uninterrupted run-through for timing and general "feel" of the episode. To assist timing, each script is liberally provided with "optional cuts" — marked passages of dialogue which, if time runs short, may be dropped without interfering with the main thread of the story.
>
> After this run-through, Reg Johnston went into the studio, and I could hear him briefing the actors on various points of inflexion and character, all of which he had marked on his script with the blue pencil.
>
> The narrator, it seemed, was a little "heavy". ("Remember, the woman

listener hears your voice first. She must like it. Keep the voice smooth and confidential. Give the impression you're speaking for her alone.")

The Other Woman was a shade too catty. ("Just a little more dignity, dear. I don't want you to give the whole show away yet.")

The Little Orphan Sick in Hospital was not pathetic enough. ("Just pretend you're really sick.")

Quickly and efficiently the difficulties were smoothed out. It was all very companionable and co-operative. "Temperament" has no place in the soap opera studio.

Two more short rehearsals, and the episode was ready for "cutting" — making the permanent recording.

At this point, the panel operator, satisfied that his panel was adjusted to bring in the voices at an average "level" of sound, nodded to the producer that he was ready.

The cast stood by. The panel operator spoke through a microphone to the recording engineer in another part of the building: "We shall start on your signal."

Over it came to control room and studio alike — a short, piping whistle. The operator played his opening bars of theme music, and dropped his hand to the narrator, watching through the glass wall. The narrator stepped towards the mike and took up the thread of the story. The episode was being cut.

MEANWHILE, Ronnie Parr had left the army and was selling insurance. He was the complete antithesis of Grace; still the perfect English gentleman, preserving his conservative colonial manners to a fault.

If ladies were present, for example, Ronnie would not remove his coat. One day at a Palm Beach party, a rowdy guest tried to remove it for him. An indignant Ronnie threw him out the window. Then, being the perfect host, he went outside, picked the man up, and brought him in for a drink while they waited for the ambulance to take him to hospital.

IN MARCH 1946, Reg James was 16 and looking for a job in advertising. Lintas offered him a position as office boy and making the tea, which he refused. When he saw an ad in the *Sydney Morning Herald* — "Boy wanted at radio production company" — he applied and was called in for an interview.

James was very excited. Like most of his friends at that time, he was an avid radio listener. The first programme he was ever conscious of listening to — on a neighbour's radio — was *Inspector Scott of Scotland Yard*. Other favourites were *Dad and Dave, Yes, What?* and the Nyal plays. He knew the names of some of the actors, too — John Saul and Lyndall Barbour were famous — but when he applied for the job, he had no idea who Grace Gibson was.

He was ushered into her office. "I knew in some way she was foreign. I couldn't quite put my finger on it because I thought she looked Spanish, because of her dark colouring and black hair, but she didn't speak with a Spanish accent, whatever that was."

Two or three days after the interview, a letter arrived saying he had the job and would he start work the following Monday. His duties included despatch and sound effects, and his starting salary was £1/15/- per week. "What she didn't realise was that I had a birthday in May. She always reckoned I was a bit tough on her because she had to give me a pay rise almost at once."

Grace told the story for years that a very handsome boy had also applied for the position, and she was very taken with him, but she gave Reg James the job because he was bigger and could carry more records.

In those days, even the office boy wore a suit and tie to work, with a handkerchief in the breast pocket. James loved the atmosphere and the people. "We all worked in one small office, Betty Gondolf, Loris Gunn, and Reg Johnston." In the early days there weren't that many discs for James to wrap, pack and despatch: *Drama of Medicine, Here Are The Facts, Mr & Mrs North*. J. Walter Thompson sent out the discs for *Hollywood Holiday*; all James had to do was carry the discs around to the agency. But soon a second cabinet was needed.

According to James, "Grace never signed her mail until knock-off time at 5.30pm, so consequently we never knocked off until 6pm."

Grace was a power dresser. "She was always well dressed; she loved good clothes, and never wore slacks. Usually she was in a frock, in bright colours." He was in awe of her, and at times even a little frightened. "She was always 'Miss Gibson', never Grace. I never called her anything but 'Miss Gibson.'" Once when he was going out socially with her, he asked should he address her as Mrs Parr. "No, I'm Miss Gibson," replied Grace.

As was customary at the time, the office junior called all the female employees 'Miss' too — Miss Gondolf, Miss Gunn, Miss Barnard. Even Reg Johnston was Mr Johnston.

"When she made a new show, I remember Reg Johnston calling me in to listen to the voice auditions. Even me, at 16 or 17, he wanted *my* opinion, and it was damn hard to give someone like that your opinion of the acting ability of Alan White or Michael Pate." When James started, Reg Johnston was paid £25 a week. "It was damn good money. I used to bank £5 a week for him."

In those days before the advent of tape recording, radio shows were cut straight onto disc. A mistake meant going back and starting again with a fresh disc. The first time James did sound effects, he came down from the ARC studio and Grace laughingly asked if he caused any recuts. "I said on that episode we had three, I caused two and one of the actors the other."

Straight away Grace hired another young man, Doug Pickering, to do the effects; Pickering, it seemed, hankered for the country life and left soon after. He died of a heart attack in his late 30s.

Pickering's replacement was Michael Plant, a brilliant young writer who would die in his thirties too, but not before being recognised as a major creative talent. In addition to sound effects, Plant wrote and directed shows. He was on Grace's payroll briefly; before long, he was off to England but returned some years later to write and direct more shows.

Plant's replacement was Ross Napier, who would write some of Grace's most successful programmes over the next four decades.

THE panel operators were the unsung heroes of radio drama; arguably, today's sound engineers could never duplicate their skills. And while multitasking is a contemporary buzzword, the panel operators of the 1940s and 50s took it in their stride.

They controlled the output of four microphones and eight turntables, cued theme music and sound effects from discs, constantly monitored sound levels, ensured the show ran exactly to time, and cut the master — single-handedly and simultaneously. Betty Gondolf watched John Woodward at work at ARC. "You can't believe anyone could move so quickly, just doing so much at the one time. I don't know how his mind worked. It was unbelievable to watch."

Woodward's scripts were littered with notes. "As soon as I finished with a sound effect playing on one turntable, I had to rip it off and cue up the next one which was needed three or four pages farther on.

Theme music was obtained from 10-inch 78 r.p.m. (revolutions per minute) mood music discs recorded exclusively for film and radio production; Chappell, Boosey & Hawkes, Thomas J. Valentino, and Francis, Day & Hunter were the most popular libraries. Turntable operators marked their cue-points on the grooves in chalk; the chalk mark was two and a half revolutions back from the cue-point, allowing for the turntable to pick up speed. At the drop of a needle they could summon up romantic melodies, thundering dramatic passages or ominous drumbeats. Producers like Grace had to pay a "needle-drop" fee — 2/6d per item per episode — each time a mood music track was used, which was then multiplied by the number of transcription discs that were cut.

And they had to put a sticker on every disc certifying that the royalties had been paid. The ARC "A" studio also boasted a large Hammond electronic organ in the corner.

Each episode was recorded straight on to an enormous master called a lacquer, 17 inches in diameter, with a maximum playing time of 15 minutes a side. A one-hour show would require four discs. While lacquers were recorded at 33.3 revolutions per minute, they were not LP records; they were cut using a 78 r.p.m. stylus.

Many hazards awaited the engineer.

Woodward's studio had RCA velocity microphones. "They stood out for voice work because they captured the timbre, the fullness in the tone of the voice, and in those days they were hard to match." They were directional ribbon mikes, with a figure-8 capacity; if required, the microphone could have two recording "fields" so actors could work opposite each other. "But you had to make sure the actors worked across the mike, not into it. The ribbon in the mike was wind conscious, and excessive breaths blowing onto the ribbon would cause it to flutter back and forth because it was suspended between two points."

An actor fluffing his lines was one thing; often some quick adlibbing could save the day and the master. But a recording would have to be aborted if an actor over-projected, exploded on his vowels, or "popped" on the microphone. "The grooves on the master were running fairly close together. On a standard record we cut at 120 'lines' per inch. The cutting head was very sensitive to variations in frequency. It moved sideways, according to the modulations coming into it. An excessive low frequency sound like a 'pop' would cause a bigger movement or striation of the cutting stylus from side to side, resulting in the stylus cutting into the next track causing a back-track, and the record was unplayable." (In the tape era, Woodward's job was made easier. The master was cut from a playback tape, not a "live" performance. "We had a system called groove expansion. There was a sensing apparatus well back in the tape path that could sense an excessive sound coming. By the time the sound reached the playback head of the tape machine, the grooves being cut had widened slightly to allow for the excessive movement. Then the grooves would slowly come back to normal.")

Then there was the swarf.

As the stylus etched its way across the surface of the disc, it produced 1,250 linear feet of waste thread, which had to be removed before it snarled the stylus. "You had to be careful that this thread was sucked into a tube and removed. It was highly inflammable. One unfortunate cleaner disregarded the warning signs only once. He lost his eyebrows when he dumped the contents of our swarf basket into the incinerator."

One solution was to cut discs with an inside start, so the stylus travelled outward from the centre. "The swarf would lie on the inside of the track being cut, so it was unlikely to get under the cutting stylus if you had a problem with the suction apparatus." Quite often, the first disc of a one-hour show had an inside start; part two was on a disc with an outside start. The third disc would have an inside start and the fourth an outside start. The turntable at the radio station had a lever that could change its playing direction.

Cutting the disc was just the first stage of a tortuous process.

When the lacquer was received at the record factory, it was washed and cleaned to ensure that the surface was free from dust and grease. It was then coated with a very fine layer of silver, sprayed over the surface using a special gun controlled by a finely tuned electric motor to ensure the coating was even. Once silvered, the lacquer was placed onto a plating stick, connected to a moving, swinging rod that suspended it in a bath of nickel solution. The lacquer stayed in the nickel bath for up to eight hours until a nickel replica had been produced, with grooves that were "proud" or in reverse — in other words, the grooves had become ridges.

The nickel replica was called the "stamper". From it were pressed the shellac transcription discs that went to the radio stations. Shellac was a notoriously brittle Bakelite-type plastic. If you dropped a shellac pressing, it broke. Vinyl came later. The pressing cycle took up to 35 seconds and each transcription left the press with a collar of shellac or vinyl surrounding its circumference. This collar would be trimmed, so the pressing measured 16 inches in diameter.

Each pressing contained two consecutive quarter-hour episodes, episode 1 on one side, episode 2 on the other, and so on until the series was completed over months, or in some cases, years.

Half-hour shows were more complicated and required two discs. Part 1 of the first episode was on one side of the pressing, and Part 1 of the next episode on the other. A second pressing contained Part 2 of the first episode on one side, and Part 2 of the next episode on the other. This saved radio station console operators the bother of turning over the disc half way through an episode; using two turntables, they merely switched from one turntable to the other to play a complete episode.

The transcription discs were labelled and placed in paper sleeves, then into corrugated carry cartons, which were manna for Reg James, as we shall shortly discover.

Woodward also cut 16-inch acetate discs for instantaneous playback. "At AWA, we used to record the *Lux Radio Theatre* on Sunday evenings. Because it was a one-hour show, we had two cutting machines going, and we had to have a crossover point, watching the time like mad, to cross from one disc to the next. The first disc would then be turned over, and the third part of the play recorded on the other side. The next day we'd cut more acetates and send them to 4 or 5 stations around Australia. We used very heavy pickups and you had to be very careful how you used them on the acetates."

Eventually the cumbersome 16-inch discs gave way to LPs, long-play recordings with outside starts, and cut with 180 "lines" per inch. "First, we had one quarter-hour episode per side on 10-inch LPs. Then we moved to 12-inch LPs, with two quarter-hour episodes per side, or a complete half-hour episode per side."

According to Woodward, a lot of Grace's old pressings were used for landfill at the Tempe tip.

SOMEWHERE in between cueing turntables and cutting masters, Woodward found time to propose to Betty Gondolf. "It was amazing the number of radios that had to be repaired…"

Grace, Ronnie and all the staff attended their wedding in 1948. From cosmopolitan Elizabeth Bay, Grace journeyed to the Lakemba Methodist Church and then into the backblocks of Campsie. The Woodwards, like countless other Sydneysiders, lived without a car, a phone or a sewered toilet, and walked a long way to save fourpence a day. When their daughter was born, Grace wanted to be her godparent. When their son Roger was born, Grace wanted him named in the American way, John Jr. "Grace was really down to earth," observed Woodward. "There was no subtlety about Grace."

Woodward continued at ARC, but for Gondolf it was time to stop. "When John and I got married, I was glad to finish. I'd just worked really hard and I never gave up for one minute. But when I got married I thought, that's it now, I've just got to stop."

ONE Betty left, and another joined. Betty Barnard had worked part-time for Grace since the company started, lending a hand as a temporary typist when Loris Gunn was swamped with scripts. Barnard's husband was well-known trumpeter Alan Nash.

Barnard now joined full time to help out with sales. She handled direct sales to country stations while Grace pursued the big network deals. In time Betty took the title "manager", and was sent on an overseas selling trip to Africa where she contracted blackwater fever, a severe form of malaria.

As production pressures escalated, another girl — Noel Newman —

was hired to book the casts and help type the scripts. Later, when Ann Fuller joined the staff, another romance would bloom.

RONNIE joined Frank Packer's Consolidated Press as personnel manager, helping British migrants settle into jobs with the company.

Reg James believed Ronnie was "sensible enough" to keep out of Grace's business. "She wore the pants, she was the boss, it was her business. Whenever he had a comment to make, she would simply tell him, 'Be quiet, Ronnie.'" Ronnie kept his opinions to himself, bemused no doubt by his wife's bizarre world of weird actors, pumpkins rolling off ladders, and cabbages being stabbed with knives. If Ronnie listened to radio at all, it was probably the ABC.

Grace herself took great pains to clarify Ronnie's role in the scheme of things. When asked if he was also in radio, she laughed. "He'd never even heard of commercial radio till he met me."

Instead, he became the charming figure in the background. After he left Packer, he carried Grace's bags around the world, helping her entertain her clients, a David Niven persona content with a supporting role.

James remembered him as the consummate gentleman. "What a wonderful host he was. Grace needed that crutch and he was willing to fulfil that role. Every night he waited downstairs with the car, maybe for an hour, because Grace never hurried. We'd tell her, 'Miss Gibson, Mr Parr is downstairs,' and she'd say, 'Oh, he can wait…' But nobody doubted their affection. Hanging up on the phone he always said, 'God bless you,' and Grace would always say, 'Yeah, God bless you too, dear…' She threw it away in a funny sense, but he was absolutely sincere."

She was sometimes heard to call him her "little sugar".

Writer Ross Napier believed that Ronnie had to put up with a lot of implied ridicule. "There could have been another side to Ronnie, I don't know. The gentleman was always the side he unfailingly showed to me."

Even when someone once addressed him as Mr Gibson, his bonhomie masked what might have been an Irish temper.

Napier and James addressed them as Mr Parr and Miss Gibson, "because we were both very young when we started."

ONE man Grace certainly listened to was her chartered accountant, George Millar. She was not strong in the intricacies of finance, but she knew the value of a penny, and knew that if she looked after it, the pounds would follow.

Millar kept Grace in line financially. He also introduced her to the share market. Importantly, he kept an eye on the company when she was away.

While Grace watched every penny, she expected her staff to do the same. James sensed that she had grown up when times were tough, and what she earned she protected. "On the other hand, I, more than any other person, can vouch for her generosity over many, many years. Grace had that special something that drew people to her, and importantly, she loved radio drama. She was an ordinary person insofar as she knew what kind of radio ordinary people liked, and she could look at a script and see its values, and if she said it wasn't there, it wasn't. She was the only person who went about sales as if there was nothing else. She attracted important people like Frank Packer. She belonged in the smart set, and men were attracted to her charms. She had this dynamic personality, but she wasn't good looking. She was handsome, which better describes her than attractive. Men liked her, but I don't think she sold herself to anybody, although one American suggested she did. I never believed she relied on her sex to gain any advantage, and she was very loyal to the man she married, and adored him for the rest of her life."

The first time James had a drink was at George Millar's funeral. The service was held at St James in King Street. Grace, Barnard, and John Taylor, then the manager of 2UW, took him in tow to the Metropole for a few hours. He drank four beers. "I don't know why they took me, I was the office boy, but by the end of the day I was flying…"

Episode 5

From soaps to spies

1948 WAS a landmark year. Grace had not only survived as an independent, she now embarked on the first of four shows that would become synonymous with her name: *Dr Paul, Portia Faces Life, Night Beat,* and *Dossier on Dumetrius*.

Grace went shopping for a long-running soap opera and chose her vehicle carefully:

Dr Paul, radio's greatest drama of adult love. The story of a man whose life is devoted to serving the community in which he lives and practices. It is the story of his family ... his marriage and divorce from Elizabeth, the town's wealthy socialite, and his marriage to Virginia Martin ... of their children and the many interesting citizens of the town.

Dr Paul was already established in America. She bought 1,927 scripts written by Virginia Crosby, and assigned Sydney writer Kathleen Carroll the task of editing out anything that was "too American".

The first significant change was made to Dr Paul's own name. In the American series, he was Dr Paul Bock, a name deemed inappropriate for Australia in the 1940s. Bock became Lowe. Localities were also changed with typical Gibson logic. "We didn't have it set in Chicago or anything, because anybody listening to a soap opera wants to feel like it could happen anywhere, that even the people next door could be part of the story." Thus, *Dr Paul* was set in a mythical town called Stanton, where Dr Paul Lowe was in charge of the Miles Memorial Hospital.

Carroll, one of Grace's most consistent writers, eventually wrote original scripts to storylines and synopses supplied by Crosby. Over the years, other writers — Richard Lane and Creswick Jenkinson — supported her.

Reg Johnston directed the critical opening episodes.

John Bushelle was Dr. Paul for the first 20 episodes. When Bushelle went overseas, John Saul took over. When John Saul went overseas, Alastair Duncan took over. When Alastair went to the States, John Saul took back the role. When Alastair returned six years later, he was Dr Paul till the finish. "Musical chairs," Duncan called it. As Dr Paul he earned £1/10/- an episode because he was the star. "In all those years, Dr Paul never opened his Gladstone bag, and certainly never conducted any procedure." Similar musical chairs were played with the role of Virginia Martin. Dinah Shearing was the original Virginia; when she stepped out of the show, Joan Lord, June Salter and finally Lynne Murphy replaced her.

When Grace had an audition disc she was happy with, it was played to Lintas, the "house" advertising agency of the mighty Lever Bros.

Lintas snapped up the national Australian rights to *Dr Paul* for Pepsodent toothpaste, paying £40 an episode, and earning 7.5% agency commission. Gibson's supplied six transcription discs of each episode, which the agency distributed. After playing, the discs were returned to Gibson's.

Dr Paul began its epic run in 1948, four mornings a week on a 40-station network selected by Lintas to deliver the maximum number of housewives around Australia: 2UW Sydney, 2KO Newcastle, 2LM Lismore, 2KA Katoomba, 2GZ Orange, 2WL Wollongong, 2AY Albury, 2LG Lithgow, 2BH Broken Hill, 2CA Canberra, 2KM Kempsey, 2TM Tamworth, 2MW Murwillumbah, 2WG Wagga, 2GF Grafton, 2NZ

Inverell; 3DB Melbourne, 3BO Bendigo, 3BA Ballarat, 3TR Sale, 3SR Shepparton, 3UL Warragul, 3HA Hamilton, 3MA Mildura; 4BK Brisbane, 4CA Cairns, 4BU Bundaberg, 4MK Mackay, 4RO Rockhampton, 4IP Ipswich, 4MB Maryborough, 4GY Gympie, 4TO Townsville; 5AD Adelaide; 6IX Perth, 6TZ Bunbury (Dardanup), 6KG Kalgoorlie; 7HT Hobart, 7EX Launceston, 7BU Burnie.

As the show progressed, Lintas grew disenchanted. The contract was abruptly cancelled. A final episode — episode 159 — was recorded. Michael Plant, who had taken over from Reg Johnston, put virtually all the characters into a car and sent them over a cliff.

At the last minute the show was sold to Fidelity Radio, a subsidiary of 2UW, which cobbled together a distribution deal involving 20 stations around Australia including the same capital city stations from the Lintas contract. Episode 159 was hastily rewritten and rerecorded, and the old master destroyed to prevent the car crash ever going to air by error.

After a year, Lintas had a change of heart.

This time it bought both the national Australian and New Zealand rights. By 1954 it was paying £47/10/- an episode, climbing to £50 an episode in 1956. By 1957, despite the fact that more television stations were opening every month, the annual contract with Lintas was worth £10,400.

The good doctor had become Lintas's man. Lintas South Africa bought the programme for £7/19/- an episode, starting back at episode 1. Lintas then bought the show for Fiji, paying £1 an episode.

Curiously, the West Indies had been playing the American episodes of *Dr Paul*. When the American show ceased production, the story had reached well over 800 episodes. The West Indies switched to the Australian recordings, only to discover that because the Australian scripts moved faster, they were picking up essentially the same story at episode 620, with a special introduction explaining all the changes to names and localities.

More overseas sales rolled in. British-based broadcaster Overseas Rediffusion bought the show for Jamaica, Trinidad, Barbados, and British Guyana on behalf of Ovaltine. Singapore signed on, too.

Grace always had an eye for publicity. She regularly sent photographs of her stars to the stations. Often the shots were posed in costume. She was surprised one day when a letter arrived from a West Indies station requesting that photographs not be sent. Apparently their listeners thought that all the actors were black!

Before long Grace had managed to obtain another four offices in Savoy House on the same floor.

ANOTHER of Grace's earliest daytime quarter-hour serials — *The Story of Mary Lane* — can boast one of radio drama's most convoluted histories.

It commenced on 2UW in January 1950. After 208 episodes, its title was changed to *Wakefield: The Home of Mary Lane*. Then, after another 208 episodes, its title was changed yet again: it became *Aunt Mary*, its original US title, and continued for 1,724 episodes. Special openings were provided so that stations could select the title they preferred.

Reg James believes that changes in sponsors most likely led to the changes in title. But whatever the reason, the show had to go on. After all, Grace had purchased 2,000 American scripts and they *had* to be used!

AUSTRALIA was in love with radio drama. By the end of the 1940s, 100 commercial radio stations were playing 20,000 separate episodes every week to an audience of several million people. 2UW Sydney held the record: a solid block of 12 different serials played from 9 a.m. until 12.30 p.m., Monday to Thursday. And more serials followed in the late afternoons.

Why did women devour so many serials? According to a 1950 survey the overwhelming reason was: "They make me forget what I'm doing."

The survey gave a fascinating glimpse into the average suburban housewife's life. 31% gave the serial their full attention, no doubt with a cup of Kinkara Tea and some Arnotts Biscuits by their side. 26% listened while they worked in the kitchen; another 20% listened while doing general housework. 12% specifically claimed to be sewing while they listened, 7% were eating, 2% were getting dressed, and 2% were reading or playing games.

What did they like most about their favourite serial? 45% said it was true to life, real and natural. 25% said interesting and exciting. 29% claimed the voices and good acting compelled them to listen.

Daytime serials deliberately immersed housewives in domestic crises similar to their own — family complications, love affairs, with an occasional murder or mystery thrown in to add suspense. How immersed did some listeners become? A newspaper reporter called at the home of a victim of a murderous attack with thallium poison. "I can't talk to you now, dear," said the woman, clutching at her still scanty hair. "I must listen to *Dr Paul*, so just sit down and wait until it's over."

At night, Australia's main capital city stations played 35 different serials and dramas each week between 6.30 and 9 p.m.

Grace had around 20 different shows on air, playing on 50 stations in Australia, 15 in New Zealand, and many other foreign markets. Her company was the largest commercial radio drama producer in the British Commonwealth, and second only to the BBC Transcription Service in terms of output. She was the reigning queen of radio serials and carefully crafted her public persona.

Melbourne's top-selling radio guide, *The Listener In*, portrayed Grace as an ideal role model for Australian women. Clearly, they should aspire to follow her example:

> Meeting Grace Gibson for the first time, it is hard to believe she's the "human dynamo" type — and yet the amount of work she gets done

certainly proves that she is. She is busy — but not hurried or flustered. In fact, Miss Gibson gives the perfect example of a well-organised life; her energy is directed down to the last moment of the day. She reads a script while under the hairdrier, and plans the day while travelling in to the office each morning. By careful organisation, she finds time to work, to enjoy her home, take an interest in clothes and great care with her grooming, and to keep in touch with her many friends …

She is very proud of their Elizabeth Bay flat, where she and her husband entertain a great deal. When she gets home from the office she does not feel like "flopping". "I've been sitting down and using my brain all day at work," laughs Grace. "So no spending every evening sitting down with a book for me. I like to cook, to potter around, to meet people …"

Meanwhile, the staid *ABC Weekly* paid tribute to her business acumen and achievements, politely describing her American accent as "pleasant":

Some of the most notable dramatic features heard in Commercial radio have been produced by Grace Gibson Radio Productions, formed and run by a woman.

People magazine carried a story designed to warm the heart of every female reader:

Miss Gibson likes to have women working for her in key jobs, believing them to be harder workers, more sincere, easier to get on with than men, and less inclined to watch the clock …

Her appearance does not conform to the popular idea of a career woman … she wears a good deal of chunky gold jewellery, and soft feminine dresses, many of them bought off the hook on her travels for the equivalent of £10 Australian …

GRACE'S shows dominated the ratings, starting in 1946 with *The Shadow*. A malevolent chuckling voice, accompanied by a Phantom-of-the-Opera organ, introduced each half-hour episode with the words: "Who knows what evil lurks in the hearts of men? *The Shadow* knows!" Lloyd Lamble acted the title role.

Not that Grace put much stock in ratings.

"Ratings," said Grace, "aren't worth a damn thing, but are used as a yardstick by advertising agencies." She argued frequently with George Anderson whose Anderson Analysis established ratings in Australia. "What counts is not ratings but the reaction of listeners. I think you can judge reaction better from the number of people who ring up. Anyway, I've never met anyone who took part in a ratings survey."

Grace subscribed to the surveys for Sydney and Melbourne. If they said she had programmes in the top ten, she believed them. If they said she didn't, she didn't believe them. 2UE once ran a competition for listeners to vote for their favourite out of six serials. Three or four were Grace's, including the one that came out on top: *Pepper Young's Family*.

WHILE Grace could dismiss the ratings, she found it considerably harder to sideline a member of Federal Parliament. In December 1946 she found herself locked in a public debate with Mr Sheehy, a Labor member from South Australia, whose attack on commercial broadcasting had included a swipe at Grace's show *The Shadow*. In his opinion, crime shows glorified crime.

Grace's dander was up.

As she pointed out to the unfortunate MP, every episode of the series opened with the legend: "Once again we bring you the thrilling adventures of *The Shado*w ... the hard and relentless fight of one man against the forces of evil. These dramatisations are designed to demonstrate forcibly to old and young alike that crime does not pay!"

So where was the glorification? she demanded.

And, Grace reminded him, every episode ended with the announcement: "As you sow evil so shall you reap evil ... crime does not pay

— *The Shadow* knows!"

Grace argued that *The Shadow* was broadcast over 326 stations in America and was extremely popular with children, so much so that their parents often told them that if they didn't behave "The Shadow" would get them.

Then came her *coup de grâce*. The authoritative police journal, *American Police Review*, read by 13,000 police executives throughout the US, had awarded the show a citation for its distinguished contribution to the cause of better law enforcement.

"What's Mr Sheehy complaining about?" she wanted to know.

DESPITE their love of radio drama, few listeners knew how their favourite serials got to air. The web of economics and logistics was far more complex than any storyline dreamed up by Grace's writers.

Reg James spent a lifetime in the thick of it.

"If we got a national sale, which was every Australian capital city, then we certainly went ahead with a show. In those days, we'd probably have gone ahead just on a Sydney sale — UW, UE or GB — with one of those it would have been worth the risk. Then we'd immediately send the audition episodes over to New Zealand. Grace used to get her money back on the Australian sales, but made her profits on the overseas ones."

On average, each quarter-hour episode cost £25 to produce — including the script, the cast, cutting a master and pressing transcription discs.

At the very least, Grace's shows had to sell in Sydney, Melbourne, and Brisbane in order to earn back their production cost. A Sydney sale paid £15 per quarter-hour episode. A Melbourne sale was worth £12 per episode, and Brisbane £8. Some of the country stations paid as little as five shillings per episode. Fortunately for Grace, she achieved a New Zealand sale with virtually every programme she produced, so they were all profitable.

The Major Network was a different story. Not only did it buy broadcast rights nationally for five years, but it also had the rights to on-sell the show. "Major could sell a Grace Gibson show for less than Gibson's. If Major paid £30 an episode, all they were interested in was recouping their £30. They would sell episodes for as little as 4/- each and we couldn't do anything about it. After five years we'd get the rights back, and then it'd be a whole new ball game."

The production cost of every episode was finely calibrated.

Casts were kept to a minimum. Grace never allowed more than six actors in any quarter-hour episode. And one or more of them had to double as minor characters — a waiter, a taxi driver, a bellhop. If they spoke less than 40 words in their second character, they earned no extra fee. If they spoke 41 words or more, they had to be paid an extra five shillings. It made life difficult for the writers. They were instructed to prune the extra words. "It wasn't being mean because money was tight," James recalled. "You'd try to use the narrator as an extra voice. Later, the star or the co-star would do the narration. Also, more than five or six voices in a 12-minute show could confuse listeners."

The star always got an extra five shillings. In *Night Beat*, for example, the star was obviously the actor who played Randy Stone. "In *Dr Paul* it was really Dr Paul most of the time, but in some episodes he wasn't in the script. So the casting person would work out who had the most lines, and that actor would get the extra five shillings."

In 1946, the stars were paid £1 per episode. If the star did a double, he received another five shillings. James reflected, "Then there was a lot of trouble because actors wanted holiday pay, and we finally had to pay them an extra five percent of their fee as holiday pay." Gradually the rates went up. In the 1950s, the star was earning £1/10/- an episode. Those deemed to be co-stars earned £1/5/-; the director decided.

"We recorded one episode an hour, including a rehearsal. Then after a little bit of a chat and a cup of tea, we'd do it. We used to record them in batches of four. With the long-running serials like *Dr Paul* and *Portia*, most of the time we were recording with the established cast members who knew their roles, so we could do five in a morning."

Many of Grace's competitors took no such pains with their recordings. In radio drama jargon, episodes were "flown". There were no rehearsals. Actors walked in and sight-read their scripts in one take. George Edwards and AWA "flew" everything.

JAMES'S official title was despatch manager. Working from his table in the main office, he controlled the orderly circulation of hundreds of transcription discs around Australia. By the end of the 40s, he had two offices full of transcriptions as well as an assistant.

Counting the pennies, Grace ordered no more than six transcription discs for each episode. (After all, each disc cost 16/- to press.) Some shows like *Dossier on Dumetrius* sold so well that James had to convince Grace that six discs were inadequate.

Broadcasts were scheduled with a fortnight's safety buffer between stations, which explains why — in story terms — the last station on the schedule was always months behind the first station. Surprisingly, very few discs ever ran late or got lost. When programmes were time sensitive, such as a Jack Davey show on the Macquarie Network, 40 discs were pressed and despatched.

Each station licensed the disc from Gibson's for one on-air broadcast, after which the station was contractually bound to send the disc to the next station on the schedule. And each station footed the bill for freight.

	Playing Schedule 2UE Sydney		
BROADCAST DATE:	EPISODE NO'S:	RECEIVED FROM:	DESPATCH TO:
Week comm. 1 March	1-4	Grace Gibson	2GZ Orange
	Playing Schedule 2GZ Orange		
Week comm. 15 March	1-4	2UE Sydney	2DU Dubbo

Airfreight, rail and parcel post were used. If a country station finished playing a disc on Thursday morning, it had to be packed and wrapped by Friday latest and sent to the next station.

"It worked a treat," said James. "Everyone was very disciplined."

And to save Grace even more pennies, James recycled all the corrugated cardboard packaging that came with the pressings from the Australian Record Company. He taped the Gibson label over the ARC label. When stations returned discs after broadcast, their packaging was used again too. "We charged the stations for packing as well as freight — 4/6d freight plus 2/- packing." Years later, when Grace sold the company, the new owner's accountant rang James. "This is ridiculous," he said. "I was going through all your figures, and you're making a profit out of packing."

Discs were air freighted to New Zealand and South Africa, and did not have to be returned. Discs for other countries had to be shipped back at the stations' cost.

Discs were only destroyed as a last resort. Mostly they were returned in good condition, but there were exceptions. One day in 1953, Wally Grant, the owner of 2DU Dubbo, arrived at Grace Gibson's office and left a stack of transcriptions in the gentleman's toilet. James was sent around to collect them. The discs had been bundled together without protection, and someone had stubbed out a cigarette on the top disc. "I went straight in and told Grace, and she hit the roof. As a result, Wally didn't buy any of our programmes for a few years."

CRIME and suspense proved a gold mine for Grace. In 1950, *Night Beat* commenced production. Within a year of its first broadcast over 2UW on 20 January 1951, it had swept the Saturday night ratings, whether Grace believed them or not. It also benefited from following Bob Dyer's *Pick-a-Box*.

Reporter Randy Stone introduced each drama: "I cover the night beat for the Daily. Stories start in many different ways..."

The *Night Beat* story started with a mixture of American and Australian scripts, and ended as one of Grace's signature productions still heard on air until the mid 1960s. In fact, *Night Beat* was the epitome of a genre that Grace pioneered: *radio noir*. If Macquarie Plays, Lux Theatre and Colgate-Palmolive were MGM, Grace staked out a claim for the Warner Bros-RKO territory, and her best crime and suspense shows were consummately crafted stories, dark, cynical, redolent of alleyways, saloons, cheap hotels, police stations, mortuaries, and greasy diners. This was black-and-white radio, textured like *film noir*, shadowy, edgy, half-lit, garish, sinister.

Film noir had its genesis in 1944 with Robert Mitchum's *When Strangers Marry*. The emerging genre clearly influenced the original Hollywood *Night Beat* scripts on the NBC network. Grace knew the show would be a great hit with Australian listeners, especially in the hands of director Reg Johnston.

Protagonist Randy Stone was a newspaper columnist who worked throughout the night looking for unusual and heartbreaking human interest stories, "the strange stories waiting for him in the darkness". The down and out, the rich and famous, criminals and distressed children were all part of his "beat". His text was peppered with gritty lines: "This story started on a suburban train and ended in eternity" ... "This story started with a secret and ended in the river". His narratives evoked a world of vulnerability: "The night's just about washed up, the sky's getting that tell-tale grey around the edges" ... "It's the time when darkness can hide the ugliness of dirt and misery, or the gloom can make it worse" ... "When some little thing that today caused fear, tonight can build into despair".

It was perhaps the show that Grace loved most. It ran for eight years with the same sponsor, Stedman Henderson Sweets, manufacturers of Minties, Jaffas, and Fantales. It began with Alan White as Randy

Stone, the unanimous choice because of the sensitivity and sympathy he brought to the role, and certainly Grace's favourite actor. But when White announced he was leaving for England, Grace was in a quandary. Should she stop production or find a replacement star? The sponsor was adamant. *Night Beat* must continue. Sydney-based American actor Harp McGuire took over and was an immediate success.

In all, 442 episodes were produced. Alan White starred in 164 of them, Harp McGuire in 278. Supporting casts included Rod Taylor, Lyndall Barbour, John Meillon, Dinah Shearing, Charles Tingwell and June Salter.

Peter Yeldham, Ross Napier, Michael Noonan, Don Haring and others wrote 400 scripts. Interestingly, some local scriptwriters could not understand the difference between a columnist and a private detective.

Alan White affectionately recalled playing Randy Stone. "*Night Beat* is among my most favourite memories, and with Grace and Reg Johnston's instinct, enthusiasm and talent, it was a winner from the very first show."

While White busily pursued an acting career in London, McGuire reportedly died a lonely death. As Randy Stone might well have put it, "His story had started in a Sydney studio and ended under a bridge in America." McGuire, whose voice once held Australian audiences spellbound, had suffered a heart attack and his body was found the next day. His widow and family later returned to Australia, the country where McGuire had become a household name.

"*Copy boy...*"

ANOTHER Gibson classic that began production in 1950 would prove to be her most enduring show. Its first broadcast was over 2UE on 5 February 1951.

"*Dossier on Dumetrius* was played and repeated on more stations than any of my shows," Grace attested. "It played on 2UW about four or five times, it played on 2UE two or three times, and on 2GB, and at least five times in Melbourne, four times in Brisbane, and every country station in Australia would have played it once, sometimes twice." Twenty years later, whenever another order rolled in, Grace would chuckle with laughter. "I'd say to everyone, do you think we've got our money back on that show?"

Dossier on Dumetrius, the first of five shows featuring the character Major Gregory George Athelstone Keen of MI5, was set in post-World War II London and ran for 104 quarter-hour episodes. Keen is searching for a million dollars worth of Nazi loot. Also in the hunt are master criminal Dumetrius and his personal assassin Yottie Blum, together with his beautiful mistress Hedy Bergner. Keen falls in love with Hedy, and the struggle for her as well as the loot becomes personal between Keen and Dumetrius. The story climaxes in a disused loft above the India Dock Road in a fight to the finish, with Yottie dead on the stairs and Keen's offsider, Tommy Coutts, hanging halfway into the loft with a knife in his back.

Keen was the brainchild of writer Lindsay Hardy. It was followed by *Deadly Nightshade* with a Sydney setting. Later, *Twenty-Six Hours* captured the tension of Cold War Berlin.

Director Reg Johnston cast Bruce Stewart as Keen, Dinah Shearing as Hedy, Frank Waters as Coutts, and Guy Doleman as Dumetrius. Stewart played Keen in the first shows; Allan Trevor took over in the last two. Trevor was a harder, tougher Keen, but listeners didn't seem to notice. A New Zealander and one of Sydney's most outstanding radio actors, Stewart had studied for the priesthood and retained an affection for the Church all his life. He left for the UK in 1954, continuing to act and later turning to writing. In 1962, he won the Mystery Writers of America Silver Dagger Award for his play, *Shadow of a Pale Horse*. He wrote over 200 plays and scripts, his TV credits including *The Onedin Line*, *Secret Army*, and *Sherlock Holmes*. A devout but questioning

Catholic, Stewart's last play for BBC Radio 4 was *Soeur Sourire*, the story of the 1960s phenomenon The Singing Nun, in which he questioned the Church's stance on suicide. Stewart died in October 2005 aged 80.

When Hardy wrote for Melbourne's Donovan Joyce Productions in the late 1950s, Keen was again his hero in *Two Roads to Samarra*, which had a Scottish backdrop, while *Smell of Terror* was set in the Caribbean. Grace acted as distributor.

Hardy's passion illumined his work. His crisp, intelligent scripts transcended the genre. But he had his quirks. He loved and believed in the characters he created, provided that artists he liked portrayed them. His drinking buddy Guy Doleman was Hardy's favourite actor, and he wanted him as the villain in every show. On the other hand, Hardy never liked Margo Lee. So when she was cast in an important role in *Deadly Nightshade*, he soon had her character strangled and out of the show.

Like many writers before him, Hardy grew weary of his hero. He wanted to kill off Gregory Keen at the end of *Deadly Nightshade*. Grace quickly wrote to all the stations that were playing the show and asked if they were happy for Keen to die, or did they want another series? Without exception, they wanted another series, so Hardy was sent back to his typewriter for *Twenty-Six Hours*. Cunningly though, he contrived to have Keen shot with a dumdum shell; his hero lost his arm, in lieu of his life.

The Keen shows provided stations with some flexible programming opportunities. They could run each show as a standard quarter-hour serial, Monday to Thursday, for 26 weeks; or they could run two episodes back-to-back as a weekly half-hour show. Most importantly, as 2UE discovered, a Gregory Keen show could become a formidable one-hour vehicle to go up against the Macquarie Sunday night play on 2GB. Reg James was delighted. "Each quarter-hour episode actually ran 12 and a half minutes, with two and a half minutes allowed for commercials, so four episodes played for only 48 minutes. They had to play an extra episode to make up the hour. By taking off the openings and the teasers, the five episodes fitted the hour nicely and got us more money."

Soon, other mystery thrillers like *Stranger in Paradise* and *Walk a Crooked Mile* were running as one-hour shows.

BOOK adaptations were becoming a popular staple in Grace's production output — including such bestsellers as *Dinner at Antoine's*, Frances Parkinson Keyes' mystery romance set in New Orleans, Daphne du Maurier's *Frenchman's Creek*, and *The Strange Life of Deacon Brodie*.

2UW particularly liked them, and in the late 1940s, played fifteen-minute episodes in a one-hour block on Sunday nights.

AN EARLY blow was Reg Johnston's sudden death from kidney failure in 1951. Alan White visited him in hospital. "He talked about Grace sending him to America for new ideas, and doing *Peer Gynt* at the Independent when he got back. His death was a tragic loss. He was only 32 years old."

When Johnston became ill, Grace obtained the services of veteran producer Lawrence H. Cecil, who had been freelancing at 2GB. Johnston had directed the first twelve episodes of *Night Beat* and twenty episodes of *Dossier on Dumetrius*. Now Lawrie Cecil stepped into the breach. Reg James remembered him as: "A nice old boy. He'd been a Shakespearean actor, a war correspondent, one of the first into Bardia in the Second World War. He'd worked for the ABC. But he was tired, his best days as a director were gone."

By all accounts, Cecil was a martinet. He kept his casts in line firmly, some might say brutally. One day, suffering a severe cold, he became convinced that actor John Tate had given it to him. The hapless actor arrived at the studio and Cecil exacted his revenge. Nothing Tate did that morning was satisfactory. Cecil ruthlessly criticised his performance, and nobody could stop him.

Cecil was eventually made production manager. He directed his shows in the morning, then retired to the Imperial Services Club for lunch and never came back. His wife, actress Rosalind Kennerdale, taught radio acting and Cecil frequently employed her pupils. Often they were very bad. However, one star pupil was June Salter. Cecil's daughter was also an actress, the much-admired Amber Mae Cecil.

Meanwhile, actress Therese Desmond, better known to her colleagues as Molly Howell, took over directing *Dr Paul*. She and her husband, actor Edward Howell, had become household names in 1936 starring in 2CH's *Fred and Maggie Everybody*.

Actor John Saul also directed shows. (His first directing assignment for Grace had been in 1946; *The Story of Flight*, narrated by Reg Johnston, was sponsored by Qantas.) When Cecil retired, Saul took over as production manager. Like Cecil, he possessed a ferocious temper. "You didn't take too many liberties with John either," recalled Ross Napier. "The actors were petrified of him." If someone clowned around, or failed to deliver the effect he wanted, Saul vented his fury. "He was a very pleasant person otherwise, but he had a tendency to brood."

Saul was a keen painter. When he exhibited a hundred of his canvasses, they depicted what looked like large, writhing worms. Saul described them as, "my f-----g guts." Grace bought one and hid it.

GRACE prospered. She and Ronnie lived in style at *Kings Lynn*, Ithaca Road, Elizabeth Bay. Rather prophetically, it was opposite *Boomerang*, the massive waterfront home of the Albert family who would play an important role later in Grace's life. *Boomerang* had been named in honour of the ubiquitous songbooks on which the family fortune had been built.

The *Kings Lynn* apartment overlooked Elizabeth Bay. Its atmosphere was that of an exclusive London club, filled with 18th century mahogany and cedar furniture, upholstered in satin damask, oyster and mushroom pink. Old silver and Eastern treasures filled a cabinet. Green leather-bound volumes of Irish history lined a bookcase. On one wall stood a pair of Chinese idols on teakwood brackets; Chinese paintings adorned another. Mrs Morgan the housekeeper arrived first thing every morning, washed up the breakfast dishes, arranged fresh flowers, and saw to the laundry. A baffling array of canned Mexican foods arrived from Grace's mother in El Paso, while John Woodward supplied fresh eggs from his brother's poultry farm.

The Gibson-Parrs, it seems, were great practical jokers. A book titled *Famous Nudes* lay casually on a side table. Unwary visitors who opened it received an electric shock. If that weren't enough, during the course of their visit, the uninitiated might discover something large and soft on their shoulder — a hideous, eight-inch long green lizard, made of plastic. Each overseas trip brought more of these jolly surprises. It remains a mystery whether Sydney's social luminaries such as Marcel and Nola Dekyvere were amused.

Not surprisingly for a Texan in the fast lane, Grace's first car was an imported 1948 Ford V8. Another American monster — a large pink Pontiac —would follow. By the time it was ready for replacement, Ronnie had convinced her to buy a Mercedes-Benz. Not that their need for a car was great; journeys rarely went beyond Potts Point to the city, to The Australian Golf Club at Rosebery and Royal Sydney at Rose Bay, and infrequently to Palm Beach. Grace and Ronnie were keen golfers. Grace, who considered herself a "poor" golfer, only played the short 9-hole courses, while Ronnie once scored an albatross (three under par) on the long par 5 thirteenth at The Australian. For some years Ronnie could not obtain membership of Royal Sydney; it seemed he was *persona non grata* because he worked in the media for Sir Frank Packer.

Grace was always keen to watch visiting US golfers. On one occasion she decided to go out to The Lakes to catch Arnold Palmer in action. She and Reg James had lunch at The Australian, and then strolled across Gardeners Road to The Lakes. As soon as Grace saw the horde of spectators and the course she would have to trudge around, she caught a taxi home and left James to follow Palmer alone.

Cricket was a different matter. She once joined Nola Dekyvere for a day at the Sydney Cricket Ground during an Australian test match against England. They took a picnic lunch. Somehow the press discovered they were there. A photo appeared in the next day's paper. It was the first and last time that Grace ever showed any interest in the sport.

With Grace's new wealth came a welcome improvement in the studio paper. In the 1940s, white paper had been in short supply and Grace shuddered at the expense; the wastage factor was considerable too, as scripts were read only once and then destroyed. For large companies such as EMI, AWA, and Artransa, paper represented a small expense whereas Grace was setting up on her own in a very competitive business. When she was offered newsprint at a good price, she accepted. Newsprint worked well in the duplicating machine, and took no longer to dry than other papers at that time. However, her actors had complained for years. Reading from a dingy, slightly brown script was not easy; besides, newsprint pages made a noise when they were turned during recording. Their complaints had fallen on deaf ears. When Grace eventually relented though, her tough El Paso upbringing manifested itself in other ways.

She went through Reg James's expense account with a ruler under each line. She once demanded all his tram tickets as proof of petty cash claims. James politely reminded her that had he wanted to, he could pick them up off the street and walk to 2UW. Grace was not impressed.

JAMES'S duties were many and varied. Over the years he became the keeper of the flame.

"For want of a better word, I did quality control. I used to listen to all the big shows, the important shows, and occasionally spot-check things like *Dr Paul*. My instructions were, if there was anything I didn't like, I had to take it in to Grace. If she agreed with me, in came Mr Director and the scriptwriter and there was hell to pay. She was very strong that way. We didn't often re-record."

Once they re-recorded a full show. "It was a *Starlight Theatre*, and bad casting had caused the problem. The director put an inexperienced actor into a leading role because he was a student at his wife's acting school. It was absolutely ridiculous. The poor young guy later went away to be a radio announcer in the bush, but he was pleased because the replacement chosen for him was one of the best actors, Richard Davies."

James reserved his strongest criticisms for the directors.

"Some of the people who directed weren't really sincere. But radio *was* Reg Johnston's life. He was young, enthusiastic, and he wouldn't settle for second best. I might be prejudiced, but when I started at Grace Gibson's we were virtually in one office. I was just a few feet away from Reg so I heard everything that went on. I wasn't eavesdropping, but I had to hear it because I was there. People like Kath Carroll would come in, and they'd have a discussion about her ideas, what she was writing for next week. And Alan White would come in and discuss his roles with Reg, and they'd go through them. Reg did the first episodes of *Night Beat, Dragnet, Dossier on Dumetrius*, and the early book adaptations. And he was a bit before his time. He made a number of programmes that were never sold. He wanted to do semi-documentaries, true stuff, educational as well as entertaining. One was called *Food For Thought*. *Impact* was about medical discoveries and human adventure. *Metropolis* was another. Grace was lucky to have had him. He was very much appreciated by the actors like Alan White and Michael Pate and John Bushelle because he nurtured and encouraged them. They were the young people, radio was their life and they were really living it, and they wanted to go somewhere with it."

Johnston was a perfectionist. He went upstairs to the studio the afternoon before every recording. He auditioned the music with the panel operator, and checked out the sound effects. "Michael Plant was a bit similar. But essentially we lost that dedication after Reg died. It never happened with Lawrie Cecil. It happened with John Saul to a certain extent, but John got himself bugged with Method acting, and he actually stuffed up quite a few shows with it."

Over the years, James's other duties became less clearly defined.

When Grace held a charity function, he was barman and waiter. In those days before refrigeration was common, he went to the ice works late on Friday afternoon with a taxi truck, filled it with ice, and took it to the Australian Consolidated Industries ballroom in William Street.

And every Christmas, when Grace sent a bottle of whisky to the Sydney radio and advertising agency executives with whom she did business, it was James's task to make the deliveries. As he recalls, "What else could it have been — but a bottle of Old Parr!"

Episode 6

The fabulous Fifties

THE last decade of the golden years of radio drama had dawned full of promise. The industry was recording more serials than ever before. And, after eight years as an independent producer, Grace took another bold step.

In 1952 she bought British Australian Programmes (BAP) from Nora Burnett, who also ran the Telecast theatrical agency, and moved into their offices and studio on the third floor of the City Mutual Building, 60 Hunter Street, on the corner with Bligh Street. The big players again told Grace she was crazy, but they kept buying her programmes.

Grace's office reflected her new status in the industry. It was a smart room with amethyst wall-to-wall carpet, sulphur-yellow curtains, matching cushions, and a settee upholstered in patterned linen with big splashes of white, eggplant purple, green and yellow. A pair of carved Mexican figures supported a row of books on a dark wooden cabinet by her glass-topped desk. Under the glass there was a photograph of "my lovely husband".

Lunches became more lavish too; Grace took her guests to the Pickwick Club in the basement. Mrs Bamford joined as tea lady. She worked only in the mornings, serving the casts as well as the staff. In the afternoon, the staff made its own.

At last Grace had her own studio and with it came BAP's panel operator Eden Rutter. Grace immediately hired a second panel operator, the brilliant young Peter Bernardos, from 2GB. Bernardos was recognised as one of the best in Australia, very quick with a "good ear". He was the only panel operator who had actually been given a credit on air; in the *Macquarie Theatre's* "live" production of *The Sound Barrier*, he had worked eight turntables simultaneously to create the effects of a high-speed jet aircraft.

Bernardos did the more important shows in the morning when the casts were fresh. Rutter handled the second shift in the afternoon. Bernardos left soon after and went to study television in Canada. When he returned, Grace got him a job with Frank Packer at Channel 9 as a director.

Now that her staff numbered seventeen, Grace installed a buzzer system to summon people to her office. Reg James was one ring, scriptwriter Ross Napier four.

"I had a fear of God of Grace, and one day I got four rings and I thought, this can't be good…" Napier went in to discover Grace holding up one of his scripts from a show called *Tapestries of Life*.

"What's the meaning of this?" she demanded.

"What do you mean?" asked the young writer.

"It's all about the Ku Klux Klan and it's a pack of lies!" accused Grace.

Napier stood his ground. "They're all a pack of murdering swine."

Grace fell silent while Napier continued his diatribe. Words like evil, diabolical, and lynching appeared to fall on stony ground.

There was another long silence before she leaned forward and said, "I'll have you know my father was a Klansman."

To which Napier quickly replied, "Well, certain Klans weren't *too* bad…"

REG James had two offices, one in the new premises in Hunter Street, and three rooms back at nearby Savoy House. The library of 30,000 discs was stored in Savoy House, from where James and his assistant Warren Cooke despatched them. The new shows were now on LP records, but the old 16-inch discs were still being used; they were stored in a rented garage in Kensington. Old scripts suffered a similar fate. Only the producer's copy was kept. It was the master script showing any alterations to the dialogue; it also had the cost sheet attached, noting fees and overtime, and whether any recuts had been necessary. Thousands were stored under James's house and are now in the National Film & Sound Archive of Australia in Canberra.

JOHN Woodward now joined Grace as her recording engineer. He would stay on her payroll for the next 32 years. By the time he left in 1984, he had cut thousands of masters.

His move from the Australian Record Company was not without reservations: "I was wondering if I was jumping into the deep end," he mused. His first challenge was to remodel the old BAP studio and control room. "We were five years behind the bigger studios, but I couldn't spend a cent more than I was allowed to on equipment."

Fortunately, Woodward's father was a carpenter. He constructed a new production console and upgraded the studio soundproofing. A second wall was built inside the original, and the cavity filled with Insulwool. The studio was lined with perforated plywood, specially curved so its irregular surfaces stopped sound "bouncing" from one wall to another. For extra soundproofing, a bank of storage shelves was installed along the wall that backed on to Phillip Street where the vast Qantas headquarters was being built. Woodward ingeniously converted a cubicle at the end of the control room into a phone booth. In a separate compartment, a telephone earpiece was rigged up next to an old dynamic microphone to replicate the filtered sound of a phone call. This device is now in the broadcasting archives of the National Film and Sound Archive of Australia, Canberra.

Woodward upgraded the microphones from the ancient RCA 44BX mikes to what was then the revolutionary new valve microphone — the Neumann U67 condenser mike. The U67 is still treasured by studio engineers, not only for its warm, intimate, sensitive characteristics, but also for a frequency response that copes with plosives — words starting with Ps and Bs. Today, it has again become the microphone of choice — not for actors but rap artists, who have better things to do than watch their diction and breath control.

By then, tape recorders had arrived on the scene. "At first we still recorded direct to a master disc, but we backed every show on tape. If there was a crisis at the processing plant and one of our masters was lost, we could recut another master from the tape rather than call all the artists back." Woodward used the American-made Magnecord, which recorded at either 15 or 7.5 inches per second. The higher the speed, the better the quality. (The massive Emitape machine recorded at 30 inches per second; for longer shows, huge open spools of tape were loaded onto long extension arms.) The early tapes, though, were of such inferior quality that one batch buckled.

All that aside, tape proved indispensable. "I remember once that Grace bought an American show called *Damon Runyon Theatre*. The only set of pressings in existence was so noisy it was unplayable. I spent six months, in between other things, recording the pressings onto tape. Each show ran 30 minutes. I went through each tape. By the time I'd finished, I'd taken out three minutes in coughs, pops and sibilance from every episode."

One problem remained. The studio air conditioning was horrific. Thanks to the construction site next door, the ducts were clogged with dust. "We had a system that when we opened the studio window to let some fresh air in, the builders pulled a flag in and blasting would stop."

Naturally enough, Grace told the press a different story. Yes, it was a small studio, she conceded, but it had perfect acoustics and all the latest equipment — in short, "everything that opens and shuts."

1952 ALSO saw Grace embark on her first round-the-world sales trip — six months on the road that would shore up her profits for the next 30 years.

Commercial radio had just started in South Africa, under the guidance of Bob Lord of Artransa. Grace inked the first sales contracts. Her shows, and those of Artransa's, soon dominated that market just as they did in Australia. In the years that followed, Grace Gibson's name would become the hallmark of popular radio drama in other parts of Africa too — Liberia, Nigeria, Kenya, Rhodesia and Zambia. With television in Australia just four years away, her timing could not have been better.

From Johannesburg, Grace travelled on the ill-fated Comet to London — "they were falling out of the air at that time," said Reg James. There, she called on the head offices of marketing giant Unilever and global broadcaster Rediffusion. Both companies bought radio programmes for the lucrative West Indies markets — Jamaica, Trinidad, Barbados, and British Guiana, now the independent nation of Guyana. They were awesome corporations and intimidating clients, and Grace — not just loud but "Texan loud" — strode through their corridors of power and plied her wares. As a friend reflected, she had an uncanny ability to attract refined, cultured men — men, in fact, like Ronnie. More deals were signed up.

No market was too small to visit. Grace travelled across to the West Indies. In British Guiana, disaster struck. At Georgetown airport, by all reports a grim little place that resembled a scene from *Casablanca*, she waited for a plane that never arrived. She was stranded. Hours later she managed to struggle back to town with her bags.

By her own admission, Grace was a salesperson, some might say a "huckster". Others took quite a different view. Sydney social columnist

Andrea dubbed Grace "a feminine creature with a man's brain". In fact, Andrea was so enamoured of Grace that she headlined her return to Sydney in October 1953:

> A woman who hasn't lost her natural earthiness is radio tycooness Grace Gibson. She has just returned from a six-months' trip abroad, and except for some pretty plush trimmings, she's the same old shoe.

It was the first of many later trips. And each time, Reg James and Grace's personal assistant Noreen Tweeddale took her to the airport and met her when she returned. If it was a respectable hour, they returned to her apartment for drinks.

Once they went to meet her at the old Mascot terminal. To their horror, Grace came off the plane in a wheelchair. When she was pushed through customs and saw her staff waiting, she said goodbye to the stewardess pushing the wheelchair, got up and walked away.

BY 1953 Grace was producing 50 quarter-hour shows a week. Production spread over three studios: her own studio in the City Mutual Building, ARC's Bligh Street studio, and 2GZ Orange's auditorium in Hosking Place, a lane that runs off Castlereagh Street between Hunter Street and Martin Place, from where the *Lux Radio Theatre* originated. The office staff was expanding too; Loraine Black and Pauline Thorpe were hired. Meanwhile, calling the casts had become so complicated that when Noel Newman left, Betty Barnard could no longer handle it as well as her other duties. The 17-year old Val Vine was recruited to assist her.

Vine remembered the frenzied activity. "Grace's company was expanding at a maddening pace, we were outgrowing the building, but we couldn't stop. We didn't have time to move."

Lawrence H. Cecil and John Saul directed most of the shows. They selected the actors, and noted whom they wanted on the scripts. Star roles were selected with Grace's approval. Vine juggled the bookings.

She had three phones on her desk and they never stopped ringing.

Whenever a new show was sold, Vine got straight onto the artists' agents. "There were no contracts as such and the stars had to be booked for weeks ahead on the same day." It was a commitment between the agent, the actor and Gibson's. "The long-running starring roles were good jobs, good regular money, booked on the same day of the week, every week for 16 years. The actors knew it would always be there. Mondays, it was *Aunt Mary* with Winifred Green, Wendy Playfair and Ken Wayne. Tuesday mornings we did 'Elsie Beebee', with Lou Vernon as Papa David. Wednesday was *Portia*, Thursday *Dr Paul*."

Give and take was the order of the day. "If an actor was booked for one episode but had a chance of a whole morning's work somewhere else, I'd try to move the programmes around to suit the artist if I could. But I found it very difficult to please all of the people all of the time."

Vine had to keep her eye on the playing schedules. Recording was usually six weeks ahead of metropolitan broadcast dates. "Sometimes when I made up the weekly schedule, John Woodward would come to me and say, 'It can't be done.' I'd tell him, 'John, it *has* to be done,' and he'd say, 'But what happens if the equipment breaks down?' So I had to allow for equipment servicing time, too."

Apart from arranging cast calls, Vine helped type her share of scripts and every Wednesday did the weekly costings for all the shows recorded since the previous Thursday. "There was the production cost, the cost of the Chappell music, the cost of making the disc. Then I went through the scripts, and worked out the fees for each actor, their standard fees plus any extra fees for reading more than 40 words as another character."

Grace once challenged her word count. "You slipped up here, Val. There were only 40 words and we *don't* have to pay that extra fee." Vine was mystified until she discovered that Grace had linked two words with a hyphen.

Like others before her, Vine found herself acquiring some curious duties at times. "The Qantas headquarters was being built around the corner in Phillip Street and the construction sounds would have been picked up during the recording. When we came to actually do the cut, I had to run downstairs and plead with the builders that we were doing a recording. I tried every con trick to get them to stop. I'd tell them that their wives would kill them when they got home if they didn't let us get on with our serials, and they fell about laughing, but they also felt very sorry for me. The number of times I had to go up and down in that lift — twice I had to go, once to tell them to stop, and once to tell them to start work again. But it was better for me to go down. If Betty Barnard had gone, she would have just thumped them." Eventually a "stand by" and "all clear" system was perfected between the studio and the builders. "The poor old Qantas building went up very slowly, thanks to the builders who were so kind to us."

Working for Grace was a roller coaster ride. "We were all exhausted all of the time, but the one thing that made us keep going was the fact that the lady never asked us to do anything that she wasn't prepared to do herself. With that sort of motivation we were trying to keep up with her most of the time. She had an insatiable appetite for work. I saw her making the tea one day because we were all too busy to do it, and she actually carried it into the studio for the actors, which got her a round of applause."

One day an executive from an overseas broadcasting company visited Grace. "Betty Barnard had gone into Grace's office. Betty used to shake a lot from exhaustion. I was 19 at the time, and when I went in, carrying whatever she'd asked for, I shook a bit, too." Going home in the car that night, Grace told her that the man had said, "That first woman who came in, she shakes a lot. And that other one who's so young, she shakes a lot, too." So Grace had told him, "Oh, all my good girls shake. I shake sometimes, too."

Vine recalled that while Ronnie was frightfully British, Grace was a screaming Texan. "They were a funny combination but they complemented each other beautifully. He was superb when it came to entertaining clients, and when we girls needed a shoulder to cry on. Grace was a saleswoman virtually, she was the money, and she had nothing at all to do with production. She kept right out of our way. The secret of her success was the ability to recognise a good script when she saw one. And she had an eye for people, for talent, though I don't know what the hell she saw in me ..."

MAKING famous radio crime shows was one thing, but being the central character in a real-life crime was another matter entirely.

Grace went into a joint venture with an American company to produce fifty-two 30-minute self-contained episodes of *Stand By For Crime*. Its American name was *Dangerous Interlude*. It was touted as the crime show that "breaks away from tradition". Chuck Morgan, the central character, was "not a cop, nor a private investigator, nor a newspaper reporter. Instead, he's a hard-hitting, racket-busting, fearless young radio newscaster". So far, so good.

Twenty-six episodes were recorded in Hollywood; the remaining twenty-six were recorded in Sydney. The two American stars were Glenn Langan and his wife Adele Jergens. Langan was a lightweight Hollywood leading man whose main claim to fame was a string of flicks such as *Margie, Forever Amber, The Snake Pit* and *Treasure of Monte Cristo*. Jergens was a leading lady in second features such as *A Thousand and One Nights, Ladies of the Chorus, Blonde Dynamite* and *The Cobweb*.

Langan flew alone to Sydney to work with a local cast that included Sheila Sewell in the Adele Jergens role, Lyndall Barbour, Guy Doleman and Kevin Brennan. Writer Ross Napier remembered Langan as "an actor who may have been on his way down, a huge man, florid in the face, but for some reason he photographed well, as some of these people do."

On the Saturday night before recording commenced, Grace held a party at the Australia Hotel to welcome him. Langan was nowhere to be seen. Grace whispered to Vine, "Where is he? Where is he?" Betty Barnard went in search of the missing star. She found him huddled in his room, shaking from head to toe, desperately trying to learn his script. Barnard tried to reassure him. "You don't have to learn it."

Langan, as it transpired, was not a sight-reader. In America, a half-hour drama took all day to record; in Australian studios, two hours was the norm. Australian casts were used to collecting their scripts beforehand so they could correct any typing mistakes and get into their characters, then go straight into the studio and cut the master. Reg James observed the production. "Langan made a mess of the recordings."

Grace's problems were just beginning.

In all the excitement of mounting a joint production with America, she had overlooked one detail. At that time, foreign radio programmes could not be imported into Australia. And when Grace carried the discs of the first 26 episodes under her arm into Sydney airport she had broken the law. Admittedly nobody had asked her about them, and nobody had stopped her. But the law was the law.

Ironically, one of Grace's best friends blew the whistle — the manager of a Sydney station. Having failed to secure the programme for his own station, he reported her to Customs. Customs investigators were told the shows had come in by parcel post and that Reg James had cleared them. An inspector spent a lot of time with James, checking through the company's shipping documents and looking for the packages. After a couple of weeks, Grace decided to confess. She phoned Customs. It was an embarrassing moment and she was fined £200. James was called down to Customs headquarters and carpeted. "The inspectors understood my position as an employee and were lenient," he recalled.

The revengeful station manager didn't know how lucky he was. The show was atrocious.

Ross Napier shuddered when he heard them. "Goddamnit, she *had* to smuggle them in. They were the worst shows. They were rock bottom. They were so bad that in one of them Glenn Langan got murdered *twice!*" When Napier tried to change the scripts, Grace threw them back at him and said, "You can't do that, these are *American* scripts!"

Grace threw Napier off the series for insubordination. Instead he was demoted to sound effects, which he loved doing. "One day veteran actor Lou Vernon, better known as the star of *Doctor Mac*, came in to play the lead opposite Glenn Langan in one episode. The script didn't make the first bit of sense and poor old Lou got into so much trouble, he didn't know where he was."

Stand By For Crime commenced on 2UE on 5 December 1953 and paid £35 an episode. The sponsor was Elizabeth French Salons. It was sold in Melbourne, Brisbane and New Zealand, after which it sank into blessed oblivion.

MEANWHILE, Lever Bros were so happy with *Dr Paul* that they bought *Portia Faces Life*.

Arguably Grace's most iconic soap opera, *Portia* started her marathon innings in April 1954. Grace's catalogue proclaimed:

> This is a story taken from the heart of every woman who has ever dared to love ... COMPLETELY. Portia Manning is as capable as she is beautiful ... she is an outstanding lawyer engaged in a constant struggle to stay out of professional life in order to make a home for her husband and son, Dickie ... but somehow she always seems to be involved in an interesting court case. Walter Manning, a writer of great ability, truly loves Portia and Dickie, yet he finds it difficult to settle down because of his love for the pace and excitement of high adventure ... and then there is the glamorous and talented Leslie Palmer ...

The first scripts were American, written by Mona Kent and adapted for Australia by Kath Carroll. When they ran out, Australian writers such as Coral Lansbury took over.

Actress Lyndall Barbour played courageous lawyer Portia Manning for all but six months of the show's eighteen-year run. When Barbour wanted to take a trip overseas, Grace flew into a panic. "Tell her I've seen the world and it's not *worth* it!"

When the actor who played Walter Manning also took leave from the show, the writer conveniently despatched Walter to Ankara in Turkey. Grace was spared the bother of hiring a substitute.

THEN, premiering in July of that year, came *Life Can Be Beautiful*, known in the trade as "Elsie Beebee". From Grace's catalogue we learn that the show was

> Reproduced from American scripts which were broadcast over the NBC Network for 17 years. It is a lovable story about Papa David Solomon, who runs a second-hand bookstore into which a teenage slum girl named Chichi ran to escape from a hoodlum. Papa David gave her shelter in the small back room of his shop and there she stayed for five years. It is a story that audiences throughout the world have taken to their hearts. Papa David's warmth and wisdom are a great comfort to listeners who thirst for inspirational things.

The serial starred Lou Vernon as Papa David, with Amber Mae Cecil and Roger Climpson in supporting roles.

CHRISTMAS lunch at the American Club, where Grace had been a foundation member, was a company tradition. Ross Napier and Reg James always had a couple of beers beforehand, because she was so mean with the liquor. "She was the most ungracious hostess," said Napier. "If you ordered a second drink she'd say, 'But, Ross, you've had one already.'"

At one lunch, Grace commanded Napier to sit on one side of her and John Saul the other. They were enjoying pride of place until Grace summarily announced: "We will now all change places." And Saul, under his breath, said, "Well, f--k her, I'm going home."

Saul's wife, actress Georgie Sterling, couldn't stand most of the people there. She invariably sat next to James.

The brightest occasions were when Grace's mother came over from Texas, and another when her sister Bertha joined in. James and Napier took them aside before lunch. "We told both of them about Grace's meanness with liquor and arranged for them to order more wine." Despite her diminutive size, Grace's mother was very dominant. Much to everyone's surprise, she bossed Grace around. Napier said she had a "cross-the-border" mouth. He used her as the basis for a diabolical character called Aunt Della, which he wrote into *Portia Faces Life*. "Of course I never told Grace that," he admitted.

Grace also forbade James to smoke at lunch. She confiscated his cigarettes and proceeded to smoke them herself. "She didn't smoke," James protested, "but she smoked mine!"

One year Val Vine was told to bring her son along. "We were in a private room. Ronnie stood up to make a speech. He said, 'Probably the most beautiful thing today is that Grace and I are surrounded by our real family, our staff, and isn't it lovely that now they have children of their own.' And Grace was looking at my son, who was her godson."

Grace and Ronnie both favoured the same drinks, either gin and tonic or Scotch. Ronnie had the occasional beer, and enjoyed a good wine, invariably a white. At her penthouse parties, her staff was served Australian champagne while she and Ronnie drank French. One night, Grace saw everyone to the door. The usually sedate Noreen Tweeddale was drunk. As the door was closing she called, "Thank you, and up your bum."

While Grace treasured her socialite friends, she was equally at home with office boys. Yet in other ways she was a snob. After all her years in Sydney, she had never travelled on a train (that adventure awaited her in the future!), and only once had she ventured into the deepest, darkest suburbs — for John Woodward's wedding in Campsie. Other than a trip to Dubbo to see Ronnie in an army camp, and a stay in the Hordern family home in Bowral, she had never been to the country. Perhaps, James reasoned, she'd seen enough of farms in El Paso to last her a lifetime.

Grace wore her snobbishness with a curious innocence. One evening, when she was dining within the exclusive confines of the American Club in Sydney, she looked up and saw actor Alastair Duncan walking in. "Alastair," she exclaimed in horror, "what are *you* doing here?"

THE studio closed down for about three weeks over Christmas so the actors could have a holiday. Reg James stayed on duty. "Grace forgot that the company's business was with radio stations, not just the casts and writers. Many of our overseas clients didn't treat Christmas the same way as we did."

Grace, however, was concerned that those left running the office — namely Reg James — had nothing to do. So for many Christmases, James's job was to paint the office. One year he was up on the ladder painting when the phone rang. It was Grace, with the news that Noreen Tweeddale had gone to Tasmania for her holidays and fallen ill; she would not be able to get back in time to do the accounts at the end of the month. Grace said calmly, "Well, Reg, you're holding the fort, so you'll just have to do them."

So James continued painting, and while each coat dried he did the accounts.

GRACE'S distrust of audience ratings became Holy Writ. "We Gibson Girls didn't put much head nor heart into any of the ratings," attested Val Vine. "We judged our success by the phone calls that the stations received from listeners. When Lyndall Barbour went overseas and was replaced by another *Portia*, the calls came flooding in. One of the things

Grace would say is that nobody had ever asked *her* to be in a survey!"

Once a huge box arrived on Vine's desk. She opened it to discover a wedding cake. She called Betty Barnard.

"Who's this for?"

Barnard was equally mystified. The cake had been correctly addressed, but nobody on the staff was getting married.

Before the day was through, three more cakes were delivered. By that time, Barnard's suspicions increased. "Let's have a look and see what's gone to air."

Sure enough, when they sifted through the files, the mystery was solved. The episode of *Dr Paul* announcing the hero's forthcoming wedding to Virginia, recorded weeks previously, had been broadcast that very morning in Sydney.

And when Dr Paul's baby was born, layettes poured in. The cakes went to Sydney Hospital, which was just up the road from Hunter Street, and the layettes to St Margaret's.

According to Vine, the story had a bizarre footnote. "When Dr Paul did marry Virginia, the marriage ceremony itself was unacceptable to the New Zealand Broadcasting Corporation. The episode was never played." The NZBC, in fact, recorded its own wedding ceremony.

On another occasion, an old lady left actress Dinah Shearing money in her Will. Shearing did not want to take it. Vine said to her, "Have you ever thought how lonely that woman might have been, and the sheer joy you must have brought to her life?"

The amount of pleasure radio serials gave to listeners was incalculable, and beyond the scope of any ratings survey to record.

REG James made his first sales trip in 1954. It was a hard journey, driving around New South Wales and up into southern Queensland, from one radio station to the next, carrying 16-inch transcription discs packed in huge cases.

"Normally you'd spend a couple of hours at a station, and play them sample episodes of every show available. You didn't make that many sales on the day."

James did not earn commissions, whereas Sam Baker, Artransa's sales manager, did. "He got the credit for any Artransa programme bought one month before or up to three months after his visit to a station."

Betty Barnard had always handled the country station sales and James was not conversant with the prices the different stations had paid. He arrived in Newcastle to discover repeat purchase rights for *Frenchman's Creek* and *Escape Me Never* had been offered for 5/- an episode. "That offer should never have been made to Newcastle. They should have been paying about £2." 2NX had snapped up both shows, but when he got to 2KO the manager Alan Faulkner also wanted to buy them. Faulkner was an important customer and James had a difficult task to placate him.

In later years, Grace would tactfully dismiss Barnard. The two women had worked together since Savoy House days. As a colleague saw it, "Betty believed she *was* Grace Gibson, and Grace had to show her otherwise." When Barnard left, she agreed not to work for an opposition company for six months. Immediately the six months were up, she joined Reg Hepworth Productions.

By the time James became sales manager in 1961, the golden age of radio was over. There were no network buys. All sales had to be made individually, station by station.

IN 1956 Grace bought her penthouse in stately Macleay Regis on Macleay Street, Potts Point, for £19,000. The deal proceeded on the understanding that she could not gain vacant possession for at least two years.

The minute the ink was dry, she pushed for the tenant's eviction. The tenant claimed he was financially unable to move. Her lawyer subpoenaed the tenant's books, and he was out in three months. Throughout the acrimonious case, the tenant's wife had been seven months pregnant. "Although Grace was not too proud of what happened, she and Ronnie moved in," Reg James remembered.

Ultimately, the penthouse resembled a set from a Hollywood movie, with Ronnie's boxing cups and polo trophies taking pride of place.

Entry was through a wide vestibule and down a long hall. All eyes were drawn to two large portraits of Grace and Ronnie, painted by Judy Cassab. "They measured about four feet by two," said James. "Grace looked regal." Ten years later she commissioned a second portrait of herself by June Mendoza.

Spectacular harbour views magnified the impression of space. The palatial living and dining rooms, with their majestic fireplaces, opened out onto a garden patio. Meals for over a hundred guests were prepared in a vast kitchen. There were three large bedrooms, and even the maid's quarters had a private terrace.

Renovations cost £6,000. Most of the furniture was imported from the States, particularly the antiques, and shipped to Australia through New Orleans. Soft furnishings and wallpaper were also imported by parcel post, which meant they had to be cleared by Customs. Despite his misgivings, James was sent down to liaise with them. Much to his relief the officers were most helpful, the earlier episode of *Stand By For Crime* apparently forgotten. Grace was delighted. "Reg, I think you should go up and buy them a beer or two." The officers arrived at the local pub in relays. It turned into a marathon drinking session. By the time James returned to the office that afternoon at 4.30, Grace and Betty Barnard could not stop laughing and he was sent home in a taxi.

GRACE and Ronnie enjoyed their regular visits to the West Indies. The Barbados Sandy Lane Hotel was their favourite spot. Nassau in the Bahamas was also considered worth a few days' stopover.

In those days, British executives — jolly decent colonial chaps — managed the Caribbean radio stations. Not surprisingly, they were all men similar in character and background to Ronnie. Grace enjoyed their company, especially that of Scotsman Peter Hesketh, manager of Radio Trinidad.

As well as being broadcast in the larger markets of Jamaica, Trinidad, Barbados, and Guyana, *Dr Paul* and *Portia Faces Life* were played in the Bahamas, Montserrat, Belize, Antigua, St Kitts, St Lucia, St Maarten, Virgin Islands, Bermuda, and Panama. Individually, some of these markets were very small, but collectively they produced worthwhile revenue for Grace, particularly considering that her flagship serials ran for thousands of episodes.

ANOTHER famous Grace Gibson soapie made its debut in September 1956 on 2UE. *The Reverend Matthew* would eventually run for 1,105 episodes. It was totally Australian written and starred Richard Davies. Grace's catalogue offered this synopsis:

> The Reverend Matthew is a character whom listeners will grow to accept as a real and vivid personality. He is a man of strength and courage, gentleness and humility. His faith is Christian, in that he cannot be regarded as belonging to any particular Church Group. In the story, he takes over a church in a small country town and, from the beginning, finds himself in opposition to Barbara Brandon, who owns most of the land and industry in the area. His one good friend is Myrtle, a waitress at the local cafe. There are numerous sub-plots which add to the main storyline, sustaining drama and excitement until the Reverend Matthew preaches his final sermon to a united and devoted congregation.

WAS Grace as stingy as the legends suggest?

Often, a gift from Grace was merely a loan. She had a habit of taking things back, usually a week or a month later. She once gave Noreen Tweeddale a golf stick, then asked for it back. As Grace saw it, it was her right. She had given someone her property, and so could ask for it to be returned.

Actress Dinah Shearing recalled one of the first exhibitions held by her husband, actor and painter Rod Milgate. "Grace heard about it and said, 'Oh, I want to come to it,' so we sent her and Ronnie an invitation. They came over to the old Macquarie Galleries in Bligh Street, wandered around, had a look, and I didn't think for one moment she would enjoy anything that was there because Rod was doing strange, abstract paintings at that stage. Anyhow she came to me and said, 'I told them the one I want,' and I said, 'Grace, you don't have to buy anything, it's just nice to have you here.' But she said, 'No, I want it, I *want* it.' So I told the gallery owner, 'I think my friend would like to negotiate on that painting, but bring it down a bit because she *is* a friend.' Eventually people were starting to leave and Grace hadn't done anything about it. The gallery owner came to me and said, 'Is your friend going to take that painting because a couple of other people want it.' I went over to Grace and told her, and she said, 'If someone else wants it, let them have it.' I thought she didn't want it at all, that she was just being sweet. However she *did* want it, and she *did* take it, and she hung it literally beside her fireplace. Well, of course, you can't hang a painting that close to a fire, six inches away, and ages and ages afterwards she called me and said, 'Di, can you come over, the painting's cracking up and it's all gotten funny.' "

Val Vine would agree that Grace wasn't a generous woman in the conventional sense. "But the people who tell those stories about her tell them with love. The amount of work that this woman created was unbelievable. I always say to people when they tell those funny stories about Grace and money, you all would have had a lot less if Grace Gibson had never come along, and they all have to agree with that."

Vine experienced Grace's own brand of generosity many times. "Over the years she looked after us beautifully, not exactly giving us money, but if we'd really wanted anything she would have had that cheque book out and she'd have said, 'Spend it wisely.'" Vine remembered when 72 quarter-hours had to be recorded in one 5-day week, with three studios going full steam. "I think it was due to somebody having a baby and we had to get so far ahead. We all nearly had a nervous breakdown over that. We nearly killed ourselves, all of us. The result of which Grace sent me away for a couple of weeks, all paid for, which was lovely."

Grace was a bundle of contradictions. She could be loyal, devious, endearing, and mean, all in a single day. When told an opposition production company had had a fire, her reply was: "Nothing trivial I hope?"

Vine believed that Grace knew how to laugh about herself very heartily. "Just like any other woman she was very hurt sometimes by different things, and she used to ring me in the latter years and talk to me, and I used to think, God, you're just like any other woman, really you are. Take away the millions, and you're just another lady. She had great moments of generosity and she treated the staff like a family. When I married my first husband, she wanted to pay for my wedding reception. She wanted to put it into Royal Sydney, and my father said, 'No, it's very sweet of you, but I've only got one daughter.' 'Oh,' said Grace, 'I don't mind paying for it. I'd like to have a say in it.' So we invited Ronnie Parr to be the emcee at the wedding, which gave Grace a tremendous thrill, it really did. So she then rang my father and said, 'Would it be all right if I invited my brother and his wife to come out? I really would like them to see that we have a family here in Australia...' Mum and Dad were very touched. Grace never had any children and it was such a shame because she would have loved to have had a family of her own. So I decided, when my son was born, Grace would be the godmother. And I don't think I've ever seen her face light up like hers did when I told her. She was very thrilled. She said, 'Now I can write to the States and tell them I have an Australian godchild.' And all through she treated him beautifully. She'd say, 'If you want any business advice, Robert, you come to Auntie Grace, *I'm* the girl...'"

There was certainly truth in the view that Grace treated her staff as "her property". But the staff reciprocated. Grace was *their* property, too. As Vine reflected: "When the old Gibson people get together we all say one thing: *we* have the right to knock her, but we don't like anyone else to do it. Collectively we all go for the jugular when we hear Grace being badly knocked."

GRACE was rarely "knocked" in print. One such occasion was 26 September 1957. The perpetrator was the *Daily Telegraph's* radio columnist Alexander Macdonald, a feisty Scot who had written continuity for the ABC and scripts for Roy Rene "Mo". Macdonald had been Peter Finch's best mate before the War; he and Finch had shared a flat, clothes, and pooled their earnings in a kitchen drawer. When Macdonald discovered that Grace had imported the Liberace show, he couldn't resist reporting:

> Barely a week ago, I had a long and fairly gloomy essay all lined up on the subject of Miss Grace Gibson (which somehow teetered off into an impassioned demand that Dr Paul be drummed out of the BMA forthwith).
>
> However, just as I was about to go over this thesis and insert the semicolons, who should scoop me but the *ABC Weekly*, with a comprehensive and, I fear, overly benevolent account of Miss Gibson's Life and Works.
>
> Now, I happen to have a considerable, if not unqualified, admiration for Miss Gibson.
>
> It is due to her hypnotic influence that hordes of housewives go quietly about their work each morning (held in a zombiesque torpor by the love life of *Big Sister*, etc.) instead of running amok with a broomhandle as any housewife would be perfectly justified in doing these days...
>
> Miss Gibson is also a stalwart and persistent champion of the local actors and actresses and although there may be one or two of the tribe

who have expressed a desire to push her over a cliff, there are just as many, if not a great deal more, who have signified an intention of assassinating *me*, of all people.

Which merely proves that there are eccentrics in all professions.

What shocked and horrified me, however, was *this* blatant confession in the Grace Gibson story:

"One way to hold radio audiences is with big names. For instance, I got the Liberace show out here … I love Liberace. I love the way he says 'My mother'. He's a sweet boy."

There will be a brief pause for a string of silent oaths.

So *that's* who was responsible, eh? Many a night, tossing and turning over the radio, listening to the melodic treacle which Mr Liberace somehow manages to produce from the keyboard, I have wondered just who *was* the guilty party. Who *did* import this crass bore; this clockwork pianist who stolidly plays his way through everything, from fugues to foxtrots, with all the *rubato* of a well-oiled metronome?

THERE was little doubt that Grace could sell anything. When Grace and Ronnie went on a cruise, they discovered a radio executive on board. Before the ship reached Adelaide, she had closed a deal to sell him some new shows — and, in so doing, had recouped their fare.

But there were times when even Grace couldn't save the day. *Famous Fortunes* was a series of 52 self-contained quarter-hour episodes dramatising the lives of the rich and famous, and how they got to be that way. Writer Michael Noonan innocently included the story of the man who started the Americas Cup, Sir Thomas Lipton of Lipton Tea fame. Unfortunately, everyone involved with the production forgot one minor detail. The Sydney sponsor of the show was Clifford Love & Co., manufacturer of the rival brand, Kinkara Tea. Not surprisingly, Love's refused to pay for that episode.

GRACE'S transcriptions were distributed worldwide. Her competitors, EMI and AWA, wooed the New Zealand market. Only Artransa pursued global markets.

In 1958, the Australian radio transcription industry earned £1,000,000 in export sales to the USA, the UK, New Zealand, South Africa, Rhodesia, Kenya, Nigeria, the Bahamas and Asia. In Singapore, Grace's shows received official government blessing as suitable vehicles to teach the locals how English should be spoken.

By then, however, storm clouds were on the horizon.

Television was making inroads. The writing was on the wall for radio drama, though most chose to ignore it.

"We were riding the crest of the wave," recalls Woodward. "At our peak we were doing 50 shows a week, and suddenly this monster called TV made its appearance. In America it had already been established, but we didn't feel the effects immediately. Television was very expensive to set up so we were insulated for quite a while, but like all things it gradually started to rise."

An even more immediate threat lay just around the corner: a new radio format. It was called the Top 40.

Episode 7

A cast of thousands

GRACE had 300 contracts on her books by 1954. In her first ten years she had recorded 7,000 quarter-hour shows. She was booking no fewer than 180 casting calls a week. Dozens of other producers also vied for the best voices. Cast calls were constantly juggled. Very often episodes were recorded out of order to accommodate actors' schedules. The studios cooperated with each other and the actors' agents; it was a small industry, in a small town, but travel between studios was a chore in those days.

"When Alastair Duncan was doing *Dr Paul*, we'd try to give him as many episodes as possible in a morning if we had the scripts," recalled Reg James. "The more dedicated actors collected their scripts beforehand so they could study their parts, correct any typographical errors, and prepare their characters. Those who didn't, didn't get work." Extra copies were printed just in case an actor forgot to bring his scripts with him. "But Grace didn't like us doing extra copies. We were small-time…"

Sir Laurence Olivier once said that Australian actors were the best sight-readers in the world. Richard Burton, too, was in awe of radio. In the theatre of the mind, actors had no visual aids; their voices had to convey everything, including physical characteristics. Each listener saw every character and scene differently. Radio drama called for a creative act on the part of its audience. It was the most individual entertainment, on a par with reading a book.

It was entirely possible that a top Sydney radio actor played from ten to thirty different characters in a week, simulating as many emotions in that week as an average person might experience in three or four years.

Most stories were set in "Nowheresville", so audiences would not feel alienated. And so that audiences anywhere in the world could identify with the characters, accents had to be neutral; "mid-Atlantic" was the trade term. In the 1940s and 50s, Australian accents were not wanted. Certainly, overseas listeners did not think they were wanted.

GRACE was proud of the "Gibson Boys", a sobriquet bestowed on the actors who worked for her more than anyone else: John Bushelle, Michael Pate, Ron Roberts, John Saul, Charles Tingwell, and Alan White. She was particularly close to Ron Roberts, John Saul, and Alan White.

Another of Grace's favourites was Roger Climpson. "Roger was a wonderful actor," she said. "He played the part of Stephen Hamilton, a cripple in a wheelchair, in *Life Can be Beautiful*." Years later at a function, Climpson told Grace that he still remembered the character. When Climpson acted for Grace, he was living in Blakehurst. John Woodward rode home as a pillion passenger on his motor bike. When Climpson became a famous television newsreader, he moved to Sydney's northside to save travelling.

Grace was not averse to Guy Doleman either. As Val Vine related: "She used to say he was very easy on the eye, so good-looking. She loved a good-looking man. Goodness, she married one, he was lovely."

For some reason, which no one could fathom, Grace never correctly pronounced the names of her two favourite leading ladies. She always called Dinah Shearing "Diana", while Lyndall Barbour was "Lyndall Barbara". Even her long-serving engineer John Woodward was "John Wooded".

Like so many others, Dinah Shearing addressed Grace as "Miss Gibson", but later called her Grace "when I grew up a bit".

"I just called her Grace," said Alastair Duncan. "I wasn't a bit scared of her. I was doing a whole lot of things for other places and Grace was just one little section of the week, Thursday morning from nine till one. And that was it as far as I was concerned. The name Grace Gibson, when it came up, usually came up as the prelude to a joke. If Grace was mentioned, it was because there was a funny story concerning her, or an oddness, or some quirkiness, but nothing that was ever taken seriously."

AT THE time, quarter-hour serials always opened and closed with a formal narration. They were one of the conventions of radio drama, and actor Ron Roberts became Grace's "house" narrator.

Grace adored his voice. "Ron Roberts did the narration in nearly all of my soap operas because he had the best voice for it, so why change? People got used to him. It was just like having a storyteller every morning tell us different stories."

Roberts's wife was Hilda Scurr, herself a radio actress and an accomplished director at EMI. Later, Scurr directed *Dr Paul* and *Drama of Medicine* for Grace. They escaped the radio rat race every weekend and headed to their idyllic retreat in Bowral.

Reg James described him as an absolute gentleman. "Apart from that, Ronnie Roberts was very smart. Not only did he get a lot of work because he had such a beautiful voice, he was also very good at sound effects. We couldn't afford a separate sound effects man, so Ronnie did them all. If it was a big noisy scene, sometimes you had to have two or three of us working."

It wasn't a case of cheap labour. Doing sound effects was fun, as John Woodward remembered. "In the aftermath of TV, if Ron Roberts, James Condon and Richard Meikle were in the same show, they competed with each other to see who would do the sound effects."

DINAH Shearing was 19 when she first met Grace. Reg Johnston had called her in to Savoy House. He wanted her to put her age up a bit.

"Could you tell everybody at least you're 21?"

Shearing was dumbfounded. "Why?"

"Because Miss Gibson wants to do this new serial and I want you in it, a thing called *Dr Paul*, and I want you to play Virginia Martin."

So Shearing advanced her age accordingly. "I never did have a twenty-first birthday party…"

Then Grace called her in and asked her how she felt about being in her new show. "Would you like to do it?"

"Oh, it'd be lovely…" Shearing enthused, not telling Grace that any work would have been lovely at that stage.

Shearing found her "rather intimidating, rather loud. She was a very forceful sort of lady in those days, not like any of the people I'd come across before, who were mostly all such gentlemen at the ABC…"

Soon after *Dr Paul* commenced production, Shearing went on tour with the Elizabethan Theatre. She flew back from Melbourne every Sunday to record the serial. When the tour extended to Adelaide, Perth and Brisbane, Grace cast another actress to take over her role while she was away. Listeners started writing letters. "I had to answer 60 letters that 2UW sent me while I was on tour."

The next time Shearing wanted to go away, she went to see Grace.

"Well, Diana, we're going to have put someone in who can do your voice," Grace decided. "But when you come back, I want you to come back into it…"

Shearing gave her word that she would.

After the tour, Grace personally phoned and invited her to come in to the office. When Shearing arrived, Grace said: "Before we get down to talking about this, I want you to listen to something…"

She played part of a scene that Shearing could not remember doing. Grace told her it was June Salter. "June had done a perfect imitation of me, it was incredible."

Shearing kept her promise. "I said I would come back because I didn't have anything lined up with the Elizabethan Theatre for another six months."

Three days later she was sharing a taxi with Lyndall Barbour, who suddenly launched into a bitter attack.

"I don't know what's the matter with you," Barbour snapped. "I've never heard of anything so *unethical*."

"I beg your pardon?"

Shearing could not imagine what she had done to offend the other actress. "Lyndall thought it was appalling that I had let June play the part all this time, and then return and grab the role back from her. Grace had told no one that I'd given her my word that I would come back into it. My name stank in the business for a while, and I never quite forgave Grace for that."

As fate would have it, Barbour herself later stepped out of the role of Portia Manning for a while. Diana Perryman took over until Barbour's return.

AUDITIONS were held for the starring roles before a new programme went into production. For the serial *Becket*, Richard Meikle auditioned for the role of Becket, while John Unicomb read for the role of King Henry. Neither was right, but the solution was obvious: the roles were reversed. Meikle became Henry, John was Becket. They were perfect. So, too, was Dinah Shearing in the role of Eleanor of Aquitaine.

For *Pretty Kitty Kelly*, eighteen young actresses auditioned for the role of Kitty. Lesley Pope was selected. (Pope was the wife of Sid Piddington, whose unlikely radio show using extrasensory perception to communicate messages from one mind to another proved highly successful.) On the other hand, John O'Malley was an obvious choice as her co-star.

Five actors auditioned for the role of Joe Friday in *Dragnet*. Alan White set the standard, but was ruled out because he was already starring as Randy Stone in *Night Beat*. Frank Waters was awarded the iconic role of Friday and proved perfect, while White was compensated with the part of a killer in the first episode.

On other occasions, the choice of stars was obvious: Michael Pate in *The Bishop's Mantle*, Lloyd Lamble as *The Shadow*, Lyndall Barbour as Portia Manning in *Portia Faces Life*, John Saul and Dinah Shearing as Paul and Virginia in *Dr Paul*, and Lou Vernon and Roger Climpson as Papa David and Stephen in *Life Can Be Beautiful*. For *Dossier on Dumetrius*, there was no debate: who else but Bruce Stewart and Guy Doleman could portray Gregory Keen and Dumetrius?

WERE radio actors exploited? Not from Grace's perspective. "The players would run in and grab their scripts, get through their show, and run out to another studio. They weren't getting terrifically high fees, but the fees were satisfactory for those times, and by the end of the week they'd collected quite a bit of sugar with all the shows they'd done."

A starring role in a major serial like *Dr Paul* paid around £1/10/- an episode. It sounds trifling by today's standards, but in the golden days of radio a leading actor's morning call to record four episodes was worth over £6; another four episodes starring in another serial in the afternoon would rake in another similar amount. In the late 1940s, earning more than £12 a day, four or five days a week, was a massive income.

The ABC paid more, with arguably less stress attached.

Fortunately, the main studios were all located around Bligh Street — ARC and 2UE in Savoy House, and Grace Gibson on the corner at Hunter Street. Artransa and Macquarie were just around the corner in Phillip Street. The 2GZ Auditorium was in nearby Hosking Place. A job at AWA meant a quick dash up to Clarence Street, but a trip to EMI out at Homebush was a different proposition. Eventually, EMI relocated its studio to Emitron House in Castlereagh Street, a couple of blocks from Central Station.

Schedules were grueling, and actors rarely had time to listen to themselves on air in their various roles. Alastair Duncan went home exhausted every day. "You could do four to six episodes of a serial in the morning, have lunch, then go out to EMI at Homebush and do another four or five episodes in the afternoon. Then you could come back to the ABC and record a feature, or rehearse a play, for two or three hours at night…"

Dinah Shearing will never forget one hectic day. "I worked for Grace from 9 till 11. I had a taxi waiting, circling the block, to take me over to AWA from 11 till 1. I had something to do at the other end of town at 1. Then I had to get on a train and zoom out to George Edwards at Homebush, then come back in for an evening rehearsal with Neil Hutchison at the ABC. (Hutchison was the ABC Director of Drama and Features.) I hadn't had anything to eat all day, so by 7 o'clock I was feeling not just peckish, but quite sort of floaty."

A role in a one-hour Sunday night Macquarie play paid a lot more — £20 — because the plays were performed before an audience and broadcast "live" across Australia. Casts were required to read and rehearse on Friday afternoon, rehearse again on Saturday afternoon, and attend a final rehearsal on Sunday afternoon.

Michael Pate was a frequent Macquarie star. "There was no mucking around there. You couldn't make mistakes. We had 250 people or so watching us when we did them. The women were expected to look very attractive in evening dress and the men had to be in tuxedoes — a white or a pale blue tux, double-breasted. For the Macquarie show, the director E. Mason Wood also wore a black tux, even though nobody ever saw him, he was up in the control box." However a "live" play in the 2UW Theatre was a different matter. "With Harry Dearth you could not wear a white tux because Harry wore a white coat, and he was on stage with headphones giving you signals." According to Pate, some actors dressed better than others. "You'd get someone like John Cazabon, his shirt would blossom out of his pants and you'd worry whether he actually had his tuxedo pants on properly. We'd go and straighten his tie for him."

DESPITE the industry's voracious demands, not everyone worked all day every day. Women were particularly disadvantaged; more roles were available to men. On average, out of a cast of six only two roles would be for women. Only a handful of shows actually starred a woman: *Portia Faces Life*, *Big Sister*, *Delia of Four Winds*, *Life of Mary Sothern*, *When a Girl Marries* and *Aunt Mary*. Even a man portrayed Mrs 'Obbs!

Actress Betty McDowall once confessed to Dinah Shearing over lunch, "If I could just earn £16 a week, that's all I really need, that would be perfect." Shearing remembered thinking, "Oh, I'm lucky if earn between £12 and £14…"

Another time, Shearing met veteran actress Ethel Lang in the city. Lang had become a household name as Velvet Soap's *Aunt Jenny*, and was a long-time *Blue Hills* cast member. Shearing casually offered to buy her a cup of coffee. Lang said, "That would be lovely, because I can't afford one myself."

Shearing called radio a chancy business. When she won the Macquarie Award for acting, her bookings evaporated — the tall poppy syndrome, perhaps. "*Dr Paul* paid my rent every week, £4/8/-, so anything on top of that was profit." Shearing did not have an agent. "I was so naive about money. I honestly used to just accept what anyone paid me, and of course Grace went on like that for a thousand years." When she had children she stepped out of acting for years, but one day she did a play for the ABC. Don Crosby was directing and took her aside.

"Why are you working for this fee?" he asked.

"That's the fee, for goodness sake," she said and shrugged.

"For God's sake, anyone who's got your experience shouldn't be working for that," Crosby growled.

"What should I ask for?"

When Crosby told her, she was shocked. "I couldn't ask *that!*"

Shearing thought about it and signed on with theatrical agent Bill Shanahan. "And he rang me almost immediately and asked if I'd like to do a film. I'd done a few television things by that time, and I said, 'Oh, I don't know, Bill. How much do they pay?' He named a figure and I thought, 'Good God! That'd keep us all for a year…' I was so shocked I said, 'Oh, that's — *that's disgusting!*' And he said, 'Oh, don't worry, I'll get you more!' And he did."

Reg James called it a hard business. The sensible ones had another job. The glass-eyed Owen Ainley, whose most famous role was Alfie, the husband to Dan Agar's *Mrs 'Obbs,* worked as an insurance agent. *Ada and Elsie's* Dorothy Foster ran a successful real estate business. Rodney Jacob worked in a menswear store. Grant Taylor's son Kit was a taxi driver. "Friday afternoon was when the poorer actors used to come around, to remind you they were available. Some of them would bring the girls a box of chocolates. Some actors even borrowed from the company. Betty Barnard and I kept the records. Grace never knew about it."

BEING late was an unforgivable sin. Lawrence H. Cecil's edict for radio actors was carved in stone: "If you're not ten minutes early, you're late."

And for good reason. If one actor was late, the others saw their day's schedules and incomes disrupted.

Mostly, said Reg James, the actors were very professional and tried to be early. "If the call was 9 a.m. and the cast wasn't assembled until 9.10 a.m., we had every right to hold them until 10.10am. If some of the actors had a job at 10.15 a.m. at Artransa, they'd be chafing at the bit to get away. If a show was running late, we'd always ring the next studio and warn them in advance."

One legendary latecomer was John Cazabon. The talented, British-born actor had won Macquarie awards in the 1940s, but descended into heavy drinking after a shattering divorce. "He was always late," confirmed Dinah Shearing. "Always, no matter what happened, he was never there on time for the first call of the morning. He had a flat in the same building in Liverpool Street as Lloyd Berrell. And Lloyd got into the habit of waking him. No matter how hung over he was, and even if he didn't have a call in the morning, Lloyd would set the alarm, go into John's flat, wake him up, put him under the shower, turn the water on, and go away. One morning Lloyd didn't do it and John was terribly, *terribly* late for his first call, and everybody got *very* cross, because if you had to work somewhere else at 11, he'd made things very difficult. The next day, when we were all rehearsing again, he came in with bottles of Scotch for the blokes and big bouquets for the women, and I've never felt so mean or miserable. I really didn't want to take it."

If an actor called in sick on the morning of recording, the episode was cancelled and Grace didn't have to pay the cast. Grace only paid if there was a technical fault in the studio and the cast had to be re-called. Obviously, actors had to be "damn sick" not to turn up.

It was a high-pressure business. Actors who caused re-cuts were not popular. Val Vine believed that the tension bred camaraderie. "There was a tremendous togetherness because there was no room for error. Nobody will ever understand the incredible pressure that was on those artists — not only on their voices and their eyes, but their legs. They had to run from one end of town to the other. Hunter Street was a hill, and I've seen them running up that hill. They had incredible energy. I wonder sometimes how the devil it ever got done. But indeed it did get done, and done very well."

Reg James could always sympathise with them. "No wonder they went to the pub." At one time Lyndall Barbour used to sit in the Metropole lounge for hours on end, waiting for her next calls and reading scripts. There was no time to return home for a break.

FRIDAY was the day "the ghost walked", according to Alastair Duncan. "It's an old theatre saying for payday, and no producer in his right mind would rehearse or record a serial on a Friday."

Everyone picked up their money on Friday morning and went to the pub. They started at the Long Bar at the Hotel Australia, in Castlereagh Street between Martin Place and King Streets. Actor John Meillon was then 16 years of age and quite small; his taller colleagues concealed him in the middle of the group and went through to the Long Bar in a huddle. "Everyone bought a round of schooners and apparently that was where John got the taste," said Duncan, "and never lost it."

Sydney's radio acting fraternity was closely knit. All-night drinking sessions were followed by days chasing from one studio to the next, switching roles and accents with incredible dexterity. One morning in Grace's studio Dinah Shearing was doing an energetic scene where everyone was running and breathing heavily. "There was Lloyd Berrell, Nigel Lovell and John Bushelle. They had all been out the night before, and there was a very strong smell of red wine and garlic. We were all running, when suddenly the microphone seemed to come up and hit me on the head, and I realised that with all those fumes, I'd nearly passed out." Another time at Grace's studio, Shearing stepped into a dense fog. "I remember not being able to see who was on the other side of the studio. It was so thick with smoke."

Michael Pate abstained from the pub crawls. "They all went to the Australia, or the Durban in Elizabeth Street, and various other pubs around the place, and many of them drank themselves silly. I didn't care for beer. Beer stank for me."

IN ONE sense, radio acting was an unnatural process. Actors had to contort their faces to produce effects, or chew pencils to simulate eating, while working to each other around a microphone. A radio kiss could be achieved easily. For a peck on the cheek, an actor could just lightly kiss the back of his hand. For something more passionate, a long pause and a release of breath created the appropriate effect.

If Alastair Duncan had to talk while he was "eating", he simply chewed his tongue. It satisfied most directors, but not all. "Some were *much* fussier about eating. At the BBC, I was chewing my tongue when the director put the key down and said, 'Go down to the canteen and get something to eat.' So I ate some cake while I read my lines. Again the director put down the key and said: 'Go straight back there and get a sandwich. I want the sound of *bread!*'"

When Dinah Shearing first started in the business, she took weeping very seriously. "When I had to weep, I would get so far into the character that I would weep. But the more sophisticated actors almost frowned on that kind of thing. They used to say, why go to all that trouble? So you eventually got to know little sounds you could make, your voice would do funny things when you were upset, and you could do that quite normally. To sound as though you might have been weeping, you could always do a little sniff…"

Whenever Alastair Duncan played a scene with Dinah Shearing, he actually looked at her. "It was quite extraordinary. With someone like Dinah you could just sort of refer to the script, and keep the contact going. It made the scene so easy to play." But not if there were distractions — such as frantic hand signals from the control room. If the episode were running short, the director would be making a "stretch" sign to the cast. If the script was over length, the actors got a "wind up" signal. Either way, radio actors had to think on their feet.

Actors often created their own sound effects as they read their lines.

"I can't imagine anything that I haven't done for Grace," recalled Shearing. "Every sound imaginable — horse's hoofs, footsteps, treading on gravel, literally sloshing through water in a tray with pebbles in the bottom of it."

Michael Pate thought nothing of walking the length of a sound box if the sound effects person was occupied or had too much to do. "Oscar Lansbury at 2GB didn't appreciate you doing sound effects for him. I once asked him, 'Oscar, how is it that you can *run* in character?'"

Then there were the unwanted sound effects — the rustling of scripts.

According to legend, Macquarie director E. Mason Wood once stormed into the studio in a fury and shouted, "Why must you all turn your pages over at the same time?"

Handling scripts silently was an art unto itself.

Michael Pate perfected his own method. "Some people dropped each completed page on the floor, but I found that was not a good habit because sometimes they'd flutter as they went down." Pate preferred to slide each page down, revealing the top speeches on the page beneath. Then, while someone else was reading, he would turn away from the microphone and tuck the completed page under the rest when he was "off mike".

GRACE'S door was always open to actors. One day, Betty McDowall and Madi Hedd dressed up in their finery and called to see Grace in her office about a pay rise. After the meeting Grace ran out to Val Vine and said, "Oh, they looked so pretty but they turned out to be real monsters. *Monsters!* They wanted more money!"

John Bushelle saw Grace at a party one night. In the course of conversation he reminded her he had once asked for a pay rise.

"Oh, John," said Grace, "did I ever give you that pay increase?"

"No, Grace, come to think of it, you didn't."

To which she replied, "That sounds like me," and walked off, leaving Bushelle with his mouth hanging open.

Vine herself once went in to ask Grace for a pay rise. "That's funny you should say that," Grace countered. "So-and-so was just saying how she'd love to do your job." Vine couldn't get out of her office fast enough.

When Harp McGuire had finished playing Randy Stone in *Night Beat*, he returned to America. He decided to call in and say a last goodbye to Grace, and thank her for all the things she had done for him over the years. McGuire was in for a shock. Grace had a cheque made out for him as a bon voyage present. McGuire looked at the cheque and then at Grace. "Oh my God," he gasped out loud, "now I can't call you mean any more!"

After he had left, Grace popped out to share the joke with Vine. "I think that's so funny, don't you?" Then she dropped her voice. "Why do all the actors think I'm mean?" Vine replied, "Well you are!"

WHEN Vine was first hired to call the casts, Grace had told her not to get too involved with the actors at any time. "I didn't have time to socialise with them," she recalled. "I liked them all. Everybody was so good. They had to be so versatile and good sight-readers. Lyndall Barbour was so technically correct, she never missed a comma. Sheila Sewell, Margo Lee, Dinah Shearing, Nigel Lovell, Allan Trevor, Lloyd Berrell, Alastair Duncan — they were very big names and it was a great thrill for me to work with them."

Despite the intense competition to hire the best voices, new talent found it difficult to break into radio drama. As Vine explained, "I tried to fit as many auditions as I could into our busy schedule. Time was against me there, with only one studio. We used to be guided by the ABC. The ABC had regular auditions for actors, and unless someone had passed the ABC audition we wouldn't even look at them."

GRACE'S shows were discernibly different to audiences, but did Sydney's busy actors perceive a difference in standards, a difference in values?

Michael Pate did.

"Grace wanted to be better than anything else — Lux or Macquarie or Artransa or 2UE or 2GB. That's why she made a lot of money. Her shows were of a very fine standard." In Pate's view, every studio had its own particular style. "Harry Dearth conducted his *Lux Theatres* in a certain way. E. Mason Wood at Macquarie had another way. If you went to the ABC, people like Charles Wheeler, Lawrie Cecil, Paul Jacklin, all had their own methods, and there was a different atmosphere in each one of their productions. If you went out to the George Edwards unit at EMI Homebush, Eric Scott had his own particular atmosphere. He was a workaholic — I didn't believe anyone could write that many scripts in a week. But he was totally without any sense of humour, not the least bit."

Pate was recording a serial for Scott one day. Typically for the man who churned out countless episodes of *Martin's Corner* and *Courtship and Marriage*, it was being "flown" without a rehearsal. Peg Christensen and Babs Mayhew were at the microphone discussing the upcoming bush wedding of Peg Christensen's character to Michael Pate's character. Mayhew's dialogue centred on the fact that the man who had been jilted was going to bring a portable organ to play at the ceremony. Her line was: "I wouldn't know another man who'd come all this way to your wedding, and drag his organ through the dust."

Nigel Lovell and Max Osbiston were in the corner of the studio doing crosswords while they were waiting for their turn at the microphone. The minute Mayhew delivered her line, they couldn't believe what they'd just heard and burst out laughing.

"Stop laughing!" called Scott from the control room.

Lovell and Osbiston hastily apologised. Scott started cutting a new master, but when Mayhew got to the same line again, Lovell could not contain himself. He howled with laughter, and so did everyone else.

After frantic apologies, Scott started cutting a third master, an unheard of expense on a George Edwards show. Again, the same line produced gales of uncontrollable laughter.

Pate remembered Scott bursting into the studio. "He was screaming, 'What are you all laughing about?' And we said, 'Eric, have a look at the script...' Which of course he wrote, probably at midnight the night before, and he looked at the offending line and said, 'I don't see what's funny about that...' And he would *not* change the line. We finally got past it by Nidge Lovell and I leaving the studio, while Max just stared at the floor."

GRACE always believed it was a catastrophe when the star of a programme left, usually to go overseas. *Dr Paul, Night Beat, Cattleman,* and *Gregory Keen* were the main shows affected.

Reg James remembered disliking the new Dr Paul, the new Randy Stone, the new Ben McReady, and the new Gregory Keen. "But after one or two episodes I was happy. We spent so much time thinking when someone like Alan White was going away, what do we do? Do we stop the show? Who can replace him? Would the audience accept a new voice? It was more of a concern to the company than to the listeners. Listeners accepted a change of voice probably because the first actor had created the character and the character was what mattered, not a different actor. The listeners knew when Harp McGuire replaced Alan White in *Night Beat*. They knew there was a difference, they weren't fooled, but they accepted it because it was the character Randy Stone they were listening to, not Alan White or Harp McGuire."

Nor were the new artists selected lightly. "They had to be good, the best talent available, and let's face it — we had some of the best actors and actresses, if I can still use that term."

Alastair Duncan was a case in point. Duncan had worked with the BBC Repertory Company on British radio. He arrived in Australia in April 1951, armed with a lot of letters from the BBC. "And a lot of things may not have meant much to Grace, but I think the BBC did." He had been in Sydney just three weeks when Grace chose him as the new Dr Paul.

Duncan replaced John Saul who was London-bound with Georgie

Sterling. To ease the transition, Dr Paul was given a heart attack and left out of the show for about six weeks. When Duncan stepped up to the microphone in the starring role, Dr Paul was still "recovering" and coughing badly. All to no avail; listeners recognized and accepted the change of actor, and the tactic was never tried again.

Duncan's next role for Grace was in *Alias the Baron*, later in the same year. He starred as a young, man-about-town Robin Hood — "the snide young lawyer who uses his legal knowledge to rob those who trust him; the shady stockbroker, the blackmailer..." Directed by Lawrie Cecil, it was one of the first shows scripted by Ross Napier. The show was still selling in 1968, and amazingly still on 16-inch discs. 4WK Warwick paid $1.50 an episode, while 2XL Cooma stumped up 95 cents.

TODAY, of course, the ranks of radio actors have thinned. In the golden years, though, there were characters aplenty. Looking back, we can only marvel at the madness of it all.

Young actor Lloyd Berrell, part French, part Maori, was a staunch Actors' Equity member who insisted that Dinah Shearing hand out leaflets on a J. C. Williamson picket line. She was almost pushed into the gutter by passers-by.

Berrell was fond of a drink. In the ABC's old Market Street studio, actors could rest their scripts on a circular baize ledge around the microphone. Berrell once rested himself against this ledge and found it so comfortable that he uttered the first few lines of *Othello* and promptly fell asleep. Berrell, whose talent had held so much promise, died in 1957 on his way to London by ship. He was only 32.

Sheila Sewell was a popular leading lady. However, Michael Pate still flinches at the thought of her. "The only thing with Sheila Sewell you had to watch always was that she got so emotionally involved with the scene, she'd love to hold the person she was working with by the waist. And of course in those days the girls all had nails like talons. I was as skinny as a post then, and if you've got four or five nails getting you under your ribs — *honest to God!* She would make indentations through your shirt. Once or twice she pulled my shirt out, and I had scratch marks from her nails. How do you explain that to your wife? *'I've been working with Sheila Sewell...?'* You couldn't avoid her, you couldn't walk anywhere, and you could only twist out of the way so far because the microphone was always there, and if you rustled your script it would bugger the disc."

Pate remembered Charles McCallum as a gentle, sweet man, one of the pioneering radio actors with John Saul in the 2KY Players. "Charles had a very literal sense about everything. One day he was about to record a show for George Edwards at EMI Homebush, and he asked the director Tom Farley what was meant to happen at the end of the script. Tom said, 'Oh well, you just get shot and kick the bucket.' In those days there used to be a bucket for smokers in every studio. So while no one was looking Charles very carefully carried the bucket over to the microphone and finally, at the end of the script, when they played the sound of the pistol going off on the gramophone, *KLONG!* Charles kicked the bucket clear across the studio. Re-cut! A 16-inch platter thrown away, and another one put on, and everyone started all over again."

Ray Hartley was middle-aged and vertically challenged. His voice had never broken, and he made a career playing small boys. Once, Dinah Shearing played his mother in a serial. In one particular episode, Hartley — as her little child — had to gurgle away in the bath. For years afterwards, much to Shearing's horror, he boasted to everyone that she had bathed him.

Hartley is best remembered for his role as Willie Fennell's son Ashley in *Life With Dexter*. Alastair Duncan recalled: "He used to get very drunk at parties and sing *Nature Boy*, then he would pick a fight. Ray was 4'11" and always picked a fight with Grant Taylor, who was about 6'2" and four-foot wide. It always ended up with Grant lifting Ray off the ground, holding him in the air while Ray kicked and yelled and screamed, and finally Grant would just *drop* him."

Hartley had no shortage of work. When the Macquarie Theatre proudly produced *Good-bye, Mr Chips*, Hartley was chosen to portray the main schoolboy character. Who else had the vocal range and ability? It was a moving production of the classic James Hilton story, and all went swimmingly until the play reached its emotional climax with the famous farewell line from a schoolboy, just before the old schoolmaster dies, "Good-bye, Mr Chips." Hartley very confidently walked up to the microphone and said tenderly, with millions of Australians listening, "Good *night*, Mr Chips."

Understandably, director E. Mason Wood was enraged.

Woody himself was a character. Directing a "live" Macquarie play in Brisbane, Woody became disenchanted with his local leading lady. When he heard that Dinah Shearing was also in Brisbane working for the ABC, he arranged to "borrow" her. In the course of rehearsals, she was whisked to a salon and fitted out in the mandatory black evening dress. To make up for the lack of jewellery, a corsage of lace was cunningly attached to her chest and shoulder. On the night, half way through an intimate love scene, Woody ran out of the control room, stomped across the stage in front of the audience, and ripped away the corsage. Afterwards, Shearing asked why. "Every time you took a breath, there was a rustle. It sounded like you were under the sheets," he snapped, "and we can't have that on the Macquarie Radio Theatre!"

Long-running serials developed their own lore.

AWA's *The Air Adventures of Biggles* was renowned for its outrageous initiation ceremonies for actors appearing on the show for the first time. Directed by Scotsman Colin Craigen, it was usual practice to record eight quarter-hour episodes in three hours. Possibly, the studio pranks helped relieve the pressure on the cast. When veteran actor Tom Farley stepped up to the microphone for his debut appearance in *Biggles*, he was wearing braces on his trousers; while he was reading his part, somebody very carefully undid them and his trousers slowly sank to the ground. On another occasion, somebody put a match to the bottom of a newcomer's script. It caught fire, forcing the terrified actor to read his lines as fast as he possibly could before the page was completely burnt.

THE trouble with the top actors, believed Reg James, was that all the studios used them. "Consequently they could be heard in show after show on the same night, which was a bit bewildering to listeners. It didn't help the industry. By the time Ray Barrett left for England in 1958, he was just about ready to be banned by radio stations, because not only did Ray work in so many different programmes, but he also did lots of commercials."

Some actors were typecast.

Atholl Fleming's crisp, fruity English voice suited him for roles requiring authority. Apart from being Mac and Jason on the ABC *Children's Session*, he was invariably cast as Biggles's boss Air Commodore Raymond and Gregory Keen's boss Colonel Fentriss.

Veteran actress Neva Carr-Glyn always played Queen Elizabeth I. In the early 1950s, the coronation of a second Elizabeth inspired radio dramas about the first. When Dinah Shearing was in Grace's *Tudor Princess*, playing the young Elizabeth from childhood to her accession to the throne at 26, she was "desperately trying to sound a bit like Nessie by the time I got to that age." Shearing considered her portrayal of Queen Elizabeth I to be one of her best radio performances, and one that led to her love of English history. (Meanwhile, Grace and Ronnie had paid 50 guineas a seat to see the real coronation. "I'm sorry I didn't watch it on TV," lamented Grace.)

Ken Wayne became typecast in his slick, private eye Larry Kent persona. For a while, even Wayne himself seemed to think he *was* Larry Kent.

Shearing played thousands of different characters on radio. Once she played a Scottish barmaid, and one of the actors in the studio admitted, "God, Dinah, I didn't know you could do anything like that." A lot of the time, though, she was cast for her natural voice and not allowed to change it. "One thing that got me very cross was when people said, 'I can always recognise your voice,' because they couldn't. I never got any praise for the things I did that they *couldn't* recognise..."

In later years, Grace reflected that the younger generation of actors who came up through television and stage did not have the same grounding as those who had had radio exposure. "When you're on a microphone and you're doing a dramatic radio programme, you have to be pretty damn good to play the part, to make it sound real, to get everything you can out of it, because it isn't visual. It's all in the way it's acted by the players."

James thought actors lost a lot of their skill with the advent of tape. "They knew you could fix it and edit it. I remember listening in the control room one morning and there were eight fluffs in an episode of *Drama of Medicine*. Eight times they stopped during those twelve minutes, and that was unheard of. You just couldn't have done it in the old days because a master disc was worth about £2/10/-, which was a big portion of the £25 to make one episode. If you caused recuts, you wouldn't get work. Guy Doleman fluffed all the time. Our actors could pick up on a lot of faults, they could pick up from each other, and they were very sincere about their acting in those days. Some fluffs went through if they sounded natural."

RADIO bred a slickness and quickness that mitigated against depth. In the early days of radio drama there had been crusading actors and directors. In the twilight years, it became merely a process.

Dinah Shearing believed Sydney actors were very adept at "flying" serials. "When you worked with the same people for a long time, you could read from a script straight off. You didn't have to rehearse because you knew how each other worked."

Similarly, Alastair Duncan worked with Australian actors in the BBC Repertory. "We'd do the first read through, and the Australian actors were terrific. A lot of the British actors mumbled and fluffed all over the place. At the second rehearsal, the Brits got a bit better and the Australians were exactly the same. After a few more rehearsals, suddenly the Brits began picking up and the characters began meaning something, but I must say the Australian actors were doing exactly the same thing they'd done on the first read-through."

Despite its faults, radio drama built a very loyal audience. People knew the sponsors, and they believed in those sponsors' products. They were loyal to Rinso, or Bonnington's Irish Moss, or Stedman Henderson sweets, and could remember those names years later. People didn't hear radio; they listened to it. "They identified with you more on radio than on TV," said Shearing. "With *Dr Paul* you were there with them four mornings a week." Once a country listener met Shearing, studied her carefully and announced, "So you're Virginia Martin. I thought you'd be tall and fair, but you're a little dark thing, aren't you?"

But time was running out for radio drama.

Did the actors who earned lucrative incomes from radio serials worry about their impending demise?

Shearing, for one, did not. "I was certain television would take over, but I didn't care because I didn't want to act by that time." She wasn't sad to see the end of the era. "I was always terribly grateful for any radio work I got. I could get more money at that than painting or singing, and as soon as I got married and had children I got well out of it. But I feel rather sad now in a way because I think radio is a better medium than television. Some mental activity is required. If you're listening to something you make up your own pictures, you make up your own ideas of what the characters look like, and there is some involvement, whereas sitting watching television is very bad; I don't think it's very good for you in that way."

Duncan had no qualms about television. "It was an exciting new medium that one wanted to learn about. We all got bits and pieces of television to do, so there was no sense of discomfort about it. TV came in 1956, but in fact there were still a good 14 years left of radio. *Dr Paul* went on until 1970, and one was still doing radio plays for the ABC until 1972, 1973."

While many radio actors survived television, others vanished with the serials into oblivion.

"So many radio actors were never heard of again," said Val Vine. "They just couldn't make the transition from radio to television."

Michael Pate questioned their resistance to change. "A lot of radio actors got so used to working intimately with a microphone, with the script in their hand, they didn't dare themselves, or put themselves to the challenge, of doing stage work. Ron Randell was a fine stage actor, Nidge Lovell was very good on the stage, but there were some who just didn't make it. Sheila Sewell wouldn't face up to doing any television work. She just didn't feel she had the control to do it. Lyndall Barbour put off doing TV for years, and finally she did some, and I thought she was very good."

No transition was possible for radio's two leading "child actors", Ngaire Thomson and Ray Hartley. Thomson played sweet little girls and young boys. Badly crippled by a bone disease, she walked with a stick and brought along a little box to stand on so she could reach the microphone.

Hartley, still blessed with a young boy's voice, died at 71 in 2002.

PERHAPS Grace cared more about her actors than she ever let on. In her later years, she gave a large donation to the Actors' Benevolent Fund, shrugging it off with a characteristic Gibson one-liner, "Well, I guess I owe them something…"

The man who brought Grace to Australia: A. E. Bennett (in tails, left foreground), at the opening of 2GB's studios in Bligh Street, Sydney, March 1932.

When Grace arrived in Sydney, radio was dominated by George Edwards (The Man of 1000 Voices) and his wife Nell Stirling.

A typical day at Grace's studio: Lawrence H. Cecil and Peter Bernardos in the control room, Moira Redman at the table, with Alan White, Ted Smyth, Grace, and Howard Craven.

The visionary Reg Johnston (right) directing Walter Pym, John O'Malley and Betty Dickson in a Grace Gibson show in 1945.

Grace at work with Betty Barnard in 1954.

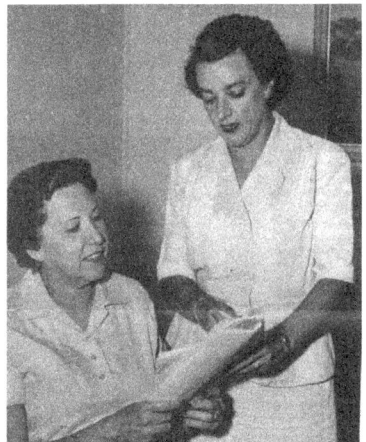

Grace with long-time scriptwriter Kathleen Carroll.

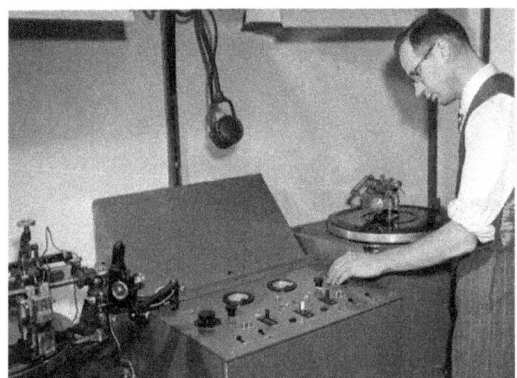

Engineer John Woodward operating a record cutting machine in 1952.

Harp McGuire played newspaper columnist Randy Stone in Grace's *Night Beat*.

Alastair Duncan as *Dr Paul*, with Lynn Murphy as Virginia.

Lyndall Barbour, star of Grace's *Portia Faces Life*.

Ron Roberts, a true gentleman and Grace's "house" narrator.

Ronnie Parr (at left) and Grace celebrating the wedding of Reg and Neryl James.

Grace with another well-known American.

Arguably the best-known transcription label in broadcasting.

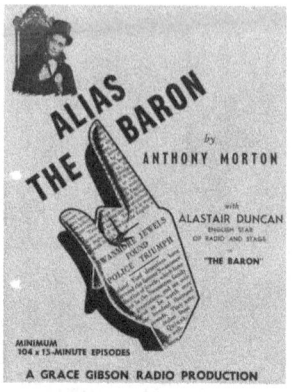
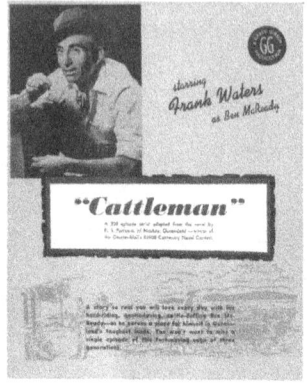

Frequent fliers: how Grace's shows were marketed to broadcasters and sponsors.

Ron Haddrick, June Salter and Richard Meikle recording *I Killed Grace Random* in 1971, pioneering the new 4-minute drama serial format.

A Grace Gibson classic, *Portia Faces Life*, with (left to right) Owen Weingott, Aileen Britton, Leonard Teale, Lyndall Barbour and Muriel Steinbeck.

John Woodward recording a show in the studio control room. Sound effects and music discs are ready for fading in and out. Note the all-important stopwatch beside the script.

The Old Guard in 1978: Noreen Tweeddale, Grace, and Reg James.

Reg James today.

Episode 8

The plot thickens, the action quickens

GRACE may have loved certain actors, but she revered her best writers. If her formative years in Hollywood had taught her anything, it was the importance of having the right script. The script was God. The old Hollywood moguls thought nothing of hiring teams of screenwriters to polish their scripts. Writers were labourers. Writing was rewriting. Grace knew the drill. She hired masters of the genre: in the early days, Lynn Foster, Rex Rienits, Max Afford, Peter Taylor, Michael Noonan and Phillip Mann; in the later years, Lindsay Hardy, Ross Napier, Peter Yeldham, Kathleen Carroll, Coral Lansbury and Michael Plant. And, as radio's golden era drew closer to its demise, her writers became more important than ever.

"The writers are the ones I can remember best," Grace once said. "Peter Yeldham, who's the top writer in Australia now, and Ross Napier. I'm a crank on scripts. There's one thing I can say about myself, I can always read a script and tell whether it's any good or not for radio. We had a lot of very good talent in those days." Asked to nominate her best-written shows, she had no hesitation: "*Dossier on Dumetrius* and *Cattleman*. And the scripts were very, very good for *Twenty-Six Hours* and *Thirty Days Hath September*."

Grace was a tough taskmistress, exercising an uncanny ability to put herself in the listener's place. Scripts were the raw material for the spell she cast over Australian audiences. Her search for perfection was relentless.

Her long-run serials started with American scripts: *Dr Paul, Portia Faces Life, Life Can be Beautiful, The Life of Mary Sothern, The Man I Married, Girl from Nowhere,* and *Aunt Mary.* So did *Night Beat* and *Dragnet.* Self-contained programmes like the *Amazing Mr Malone, Danger Is My Business,* and *Squad Room* used American scripts exclusively. But every imported American script had to be adapted to Australian tastes, as well as lengthened; Australian shows were performed at a faster pace.

Eventually though, Australian writers wrote everything.

Back in the 1940s, star writers like Rex Rienits and Max Afford commanded £5 per script. Lesser names were paid £4, and some only £3. Still, it was good money. Like acting, writing was a volume business. A writer handing in 10 episodes a week at £4 each was earning an enviable income for those days. Few worried about listening to the recorded versions of their scripts; there was no time, and for most of them it was just a job.

Each quarter-hour episode had to run 12-and-a-half minutes, or 12 minutes 40 seconds maximum, leaving the balance of time for sponsors' messages. As a rule of thumb, each foolscap page of double-spaced dialogue ran one-and-a half minutes. One episode required eight pages. *Dr Paul's* 4,634 episodes consumed a mind-boggling 37,072 pages of script!

Peter Yeldham, Ross Napier, Kathleen Carroll, Richard Lane, Michael Plant, Lindsay Hardy, Lynn Foster and Coral Lansbury were among those who fed Grace's voracious demand for dialogue. Amazingly, at the industry's peak, there were probably fewer than two dozen writers supplying scripts to the dozen or so major production companies.

Not surprising, perhaps, for even the great George Bernard Shaw had declared that radio was "the most difficult form of drama".

WHETHER or not Shaw would have agreed with Grace, her formula was simple: "Start it with a punch, finish with a punch, and let's have something in between."

Or, as Hollywood's Samuel Goldwyn once said, "A story should start with an earthquake and work its way up to a climax."

It was a tall order, conceded Reg James. "It had to be 'go' from the start, suspenseful and dramatic, and you finished very episode on a cliffhanger. It might sound unbelievable, but a lot of writers couldn't do that. A lot of writers could not write for Grace Gibson. It was impossible. They couldn't do it."

Characterisation was the most important ingredient. A hero didn't have to be good: he could have affairs, which were usually the fault of women. The most necessary character was a bitch. (As a station manager was fond of asking James, "Reg, has it got a bitch? It's *got* to have a bitch!") Good wholesome women didn't make a popular radio character — there is nothing less interesting to a predominantly female audience than a happy, well-adjusted woman. As James pointed out, "When *Dr Paul* commenced, Virginia Martin was a great character. However, after she married Paul and had a child, she was boring and perhaps proved that the worst character in a radio serial is a happily married woman with a child!"

Writing dialogue was the toughest hurdle. How could a writer communicate a meaningful glance, or the touch of two hands under a table, without visual support? Dialogue had to flow and seem natural without forcing it. When one is dealing with unseen people and objects, listeners had to identify them through what the characters said. "Pearl-handling", though, was a cardinal sin; the term originated with an immortal line of dialogue that John Cazabon once delivered: "Now that I'm standing on this carved ebony staircase with this pearl-handled pistol in my hand, stick up your hands."

Grace's loyalty to writers was legendary. Those who could start every script with a bang and finish with a cliffhanger were treated like royalty. So, too, were the writers who could sustain storylines for months, even years. Writing a serial was not a sprint — it was a marathon.

"The longer the serial, the harder it got," reflected James. "Writing long-running serials was a monumental task requiring discipline and dedication. In the 1940s, Australian writers were inexperienced at this type of writing. Kathleen Carroll, Coral Lansbury and Ross Napier were the exceptions. They could do it. Kath Carroll wrote for Grace for 30 years." The "name" writers were stars. They were featured in Grace's sales publicity along with the cast. Even their writing credits for her competitors were included. "With Ross writing most of our serials, that became very important. We'd even throw *Address Unknown* into his credits, because that made him come to life in the eyes of the station manager."

James can happily scotch one of the fallacies about Grace and her relationship with writers.

"Once the show was in production she *didn't* read the scripts. She'd spot-check them occasionally. She might say, give me a batch to take home. But when we did the audition episodes, when someone wrote episodes 1 and 2, my God she'd watch those. Grace always chose the writers. She might even give an idea to a writer. Grace would always have the final say. Grace had to like a show first, she had to approve the scripts, and then we'd record the first two episodes. If she wasn't happy, they were remade. I think the audition episodes of *Dr Paul* and *Portia* were remade three or four times. But after that she didn't really get involved. There wasn't time."

Ross Napier crafted many audition episodes. "One of the things worth noting about Grace, you had to cram everything in for the audition scripts. It didn't matter what you said to her, she'd say, 'Get it all in.' You couldn't start off a serial on a fairly low note — you'd have to get a murder in, and then Grace would be happy."

GRACE firmly adhered to one of the great Hollywood tenets: you should be able to sell your idea in a sentence.

Reg James agreed. "Ross Napier wrote very short synopses, possibly because he didn't know what he was going to write about in the serial, or just to stop Grace commenting! Most writers sent in long, three- or four-page synopses with too many characters included. They were a sure recipe for rejection. They were so complicated that Grace, as well as everybody else, could not understand what the story was all about. She didn't even get to the scripts. They were rejected because of the long synopsis. But Ross had the right idea. He was the only one who had enough brains, and knew her well enough, to give her just a brief outline. He limited synopses to half a page. If it was a book he was adapting he might just give her the text from the flyleaf, but that gave her the bones of the story."

"Synopses are notoriously terrible things to read," affirmed Napier. "They never read well."

BOOK adaptations became the foundations of Grace's output; *Cattleman* and *The Bishop's Mantle* were classics of the genre. Arguably Kath Carroll's best writing for Grace were her book adaptations in association with director Reg Johnston: E. V. Timms' *Pathway of the Sun*, Frances Parkinson Keyes' *Dinner at Antoine's*, Daphne du Maurier's *Frenchman's Creek*, and Margaret Kennedy's lighthearted romance *Escape Me Never*, which starred Michael Pate and Alan White.

However, many publishers were wary of selling radio rights in case they impeded the sale of film rights.

Grace usually paid a fee of £1 an episode to the publisher, which would license the Australasian radio rights for either three or five years.

An adaptation spanning 104 quarter-hour episodes would cost £104; when Australia switched to decimal currency, Grace paid $208. Some books had higher price tags — *The Robe* set her back $500. "Australasian rights" covered New Zealand as well as Australia, to which Grace invariably added her own territorial interpretations: "Oh, good, we can have Fiji for that as well."

Rights, however, had an unfortunate habit of expiring — sometimes with embarrassing consequences. When Grace bought *Sara Dane* for radio, nobody thought to renew them. Years later, the publisher heard the show playing on the Christian station 2CBA to whom Reg James sold shows very cheaply. Fielding the complaint, James explained how the company had changed hands since the old days; the new Grace Gibson Radio Productions did not have the records from the old Grace Gibson Radio Productions. His company lawyer said, "Look, send them a cheque, and if they accept it and bank it, we're clear." Fortunately for James, the publishing executive who was going to sue for a vast sum of money was out of the office, and someone in his company banked the cheque. "He was furious and demanded that every pressing of *Sara Dane* be destroyed, except one set for the archives."

Grace, Reg James and John Saul devoured books, looking for titles they could buy and adapt. Ross Napier never watched a movie or read a book without considering it for a radio. "Maybe half our output was driven by books," James recalled. "We all liked reading. We were looking for interesting characters, for action. Every two years or so we tried to get *Gone With the Wind*, possibly for Rod Taylor in the Clark Gable role and June Salter as Scarlet O'Hara. We also tried to buy the radio rights for James Bond, without success. Ross Napier said James Bond, as written by Ian Fleming, was one of the best characters ever created."

However, when Grace produced an espionage serial entitled *From Paris With Love*, she stirred up a hornet's nest. One of her competitors believed she had bought the rights to the Bond novel *From Russia With*

Love, and immediately approached Fleming's publisher for the radio rights to another Bond novel. When their request was rejected, they advised the publisher that Grace was producing an "illegal" adaptation. A solicitor's letter from London arrived on her desk. She easily proved that her new show bore absolutely no resemblance to the Fleming novel. (Besides which, book titles cannot be copyrighted.) As a result, there were some red faces in Sydney radio circles.

Not all books lent themselves to radio. Those that relied heavily on descriptive passages for their effect were unsuitable; so, too, were books with only one or two characters. For example, to whom could Robinson Crusoe talk for the first 50 episodes?

Some scenes that an author glossed over in a few sentences were enlarged on radio with compelling dialogue. When Lloyd C. Douglas's epic novel *The Big Fisherman* was adapted for radio, Michael Plant started the story from page 84 of the book. For *The Castlereagh Line*, Ross Napier constructed a completely new opening. In the book, the heroine was simply introduced as a barmaid in a Cloncurry Hotel during the 1880s. But just stating that fact was too bald for radio; where was the drama and intrigue? Instead, Napier decided to tell how she came to the hotel, which allowed him to create new characters that were never in the book.

Adaptations were a specialised discipline that Napier soon mastered. He kept the best-known characters and any famous lines, but invariably departed from the plot of the book by developing entirely new storylines. "Not all books had key points of action that could be built into the radio serial. Sometimes I just invented something that wasn't in the book, and I'd put that in just to please Grace. I remember *Sara Dane*. I wrote my own version of how it started. Even Grace said, 'Ross, there's too much in this!' " Napier was once assigned to adapt Marcus Clarke's panoramic novel *For the Term of His Natural Life*. "In classics like that you couldn't throw in things that hadn't happened in the book." Fortunately he only had to write ten scripts before the project was aborted. "It was really hard yakka."

GRACE hired only the best writers. And day after day, night after night, millions of Australians hung on their every word.

Kathleen Carroll was a staff writer from the early days. Carroll worked from home because Grace didn't have room for her in the office.

Michael Plant served his apprenticeship with Grace, both as a staff writer and director. "Michael was one of the best writers we ever had," Grace could recall fondly. "He was a brilliant writer. He was quite young when he died." When Plant wrote *Tudor Princess*, he delved into every detail of the life of Queen Elizabeth I. He wrote to Dinah Shearing from London, triumphantly sharing another nugget of research: "Did you know she had a weeping ulcer on her leg for the last 20 years of her life? *Drip, drip, drip…*" His other achievements for Grace included *Tudor Queen* and the serialisation of Lloyd C. Douglas's epic story of Simon Peter, *The Big Fisherman*.

Plant went to America where he wrote for the top television shows of the era such as *Bourbon Street Beat*. Returning to Australia, he created *Whiplash* and *The Mavis Bramston Show* for Channel 7. He died of an overdose of sleeping pills when *Mavis Bramston* was at its peak. Many believed he had committed suicide.

"Michael *was* special." Reg James can remember him as a very clever boy, and at times a dreadful boy. "Michael was gay, and at that stage I don't think he could fully accept it. Those were the days when Australians didn't accept it." Affairs with Burt Lancaster and Rock Hudson were rumoured.

ROSS Napier was 17 when he wrote his first script for 2GB's *Doctor Mac*. "It was 1949. I'd just left school. Radio has always remained my favourite medium and I was always passionately fond of every aspect of it." He wrote the date of his first script sale on his bedroom wall in crayon. His second acceptance was a half-hour script for 2UE's *Authors' Playhouse*. Suitably inspired, he tried to see Grace Gibson. "Betty Barnard, her main protector at the time, told me I couldn't see her unless I had an idea or a series I wished to submit. She wasn't interested in giving me something to write. I was talking to my mother about it, and she said that my grandfather had been a journalist and written a thing called *Great Lovers*, which were stories about the great love affairs of history. Mum said, 'Why don't you suggest that to Grace?' So I made an appointment to see her on the basis that I had an idea to submit."

It was a fateful meeting. "Grace was an awesome person. She had that aura about her, charisma I guess — you never felt like taking too many liberties with her. She saw me and said she'd done something similar, but it got me in the door. She said, 'Why don't you have a go at a *Night Beat* and see how you make out?'"

By that time, Napier had already got himself a job in radio. Like Reg James, he was an office boy — at one of Grace's competitors, Towers of London. James got to know him when they collected pressings from the Australian Record Company. "A group of us gathered at ARC, and Ross read us the first love scene he had ever written for a radio serial. He read it very dramatically, and we thought it was so dreadful we all fell about laughing."

Napier had the last laugh. He had taken Grace at her word and written a script for *Night Beat*. When Reg Johnston read it, he bought it on the spot. The young despatch boy's script became episode 19.

A bigger break soon followed. Michael Plant had announced his decision to go to London, and a replacement was needed. Reg Johnston was very ill and an embattled Grace offered Napier a staff position — writing and editing scripts, and doing sound effects. He joined the staff in 1951, and continued writing for the company until 1986.

His first day at work was the day of Reg Johnston's funeral. "I'd bought this awful checked sports coat and a loud yellow tie. I'd carried my typewriter in from home on the train — one of those old heavy Royals. It was a scorching hot day and I was pretty fagged out when I got to the office, and Grace announced we were all going to the funeral, me included. I said I hadn't known Reg but she said, 'No, you're going to the funeral!' — she was that sort of person. So I got hold of someone's raincoat and put it on over the loud sports coat, and God knows what I looked like, but I went."

At first, Michael Plant did not hit off with the young man who had come to replace him. Plant took Napier upstairs to the studio where he was directing *Dr Paul* at the Australian Record Company. "Right-o," Michael told the cast, "we're all going down for morning tea."

Napier was left sitting alone in the control room. Suddenly, Grace came in and demanded, "What's going on? Where is everyone?" The unsuspecting young Napier didn't think anything of it; he just said, "Oh, they're down in the Green Parrot having morning tea, Miss Gibson." Napier remembered how Grace turned about five shades of pink. "She grabbed me by the wrist. 'We'll see about that!' she said. She hauled me down the corridor and into the lift, and then down into the basement in the next building where Michael was sitting with the entire cast. And she's still holding on to my hand as though I had dobbed them all in. A bitter shouting match ensued. She told the staff at the Green Parrot that they were never to serve Michael again. She sacked Michael on the spot and he told her to get f----d."

An hour later Plant returned to the office, and cheerily told Reg James that he was going in to see Grace and get himself back on the staff. "And she put him back on," James recalled. "His father was a famous general."

At Savoy House, Napier shared an office with Lindsay Hardy. "It used to be Bob Dyer's office, and he used it sparingly. He was a very nice fellow, nothing put him out, nothing seemed to be too much trouble for

Bob. He'd just come in and do what he had to do."

Grace threw Napier in at the deep end. "I hadn't done much writing, just these odd scripts, and the minute I walked in the door as a member of the staff Grace told me I would be writing a serial called *Alias the Baron*. I'd never written a serial before…" Napier was faced with the prospect of turning Anthony Morton's best-selling novel of the time, *Meet the Baron*, into 104 15-minute episodes. To complicate matters, the central character in the book always worked alone. It was the first of dozens of book adaptations that he would subsequently write, and proved a baptism of fire. "It was an awful thing! A dreadful experience… The normal thing was you'd read the book, pick out something exciting, and the first two episodes would have a lot of action in them. But in this case a fellow called Juan Cortez had had a crack at this show. He'd submitted it to Grace originally and she'd bought his scripts, so she was lumbered with them."

Cortez was a freelancer from South Africa. His first four episodes had been recorded, but Grace rejected them outright. Lawrence H. Cecil then took command of the project. "I wrote about eight different versions of this blasted serial and Lawrie kept saying, 'No, that's not right.'" According to Reg James, "They must have been really bad if Lawrie knocked them back."

It was all a daunting experience for a young man in love with radio. "When I was at school I used to go in by myself and see the Lux and Macquarie plays. I'd get tickets, and go and watch the actors. It was the greatest thrill of my life to see these people that hitherto had been only names actually appearing on stage." Now he was working with them, writing their scripts, and creating sound effects while they performed. "My mother was against me going into radio. She was appalled at the thought that I was going to get right off the track. We lived at Artarmon in those days and she was going into town with me one day. We got on the train and sat down, and whom should I see reflected in the window but Michael Pate. At that stage he was extremely flamboyant to say the least. I was trying to look the other way, cover my face with the newspaper, but he drew a bead on me and came over. 'Ross!' he yelled. My mum had no idea who he was, but the way he was dressed was enough for her…" Fortunately, Napier's mother had no cause for alarm. Her son's scripts were so neat and clean, all the girls wanted to type them — and one girl in particular, Ann Fuller. Two years later, she and Napier got married.

Napier worked closely with Grace. "When I was doing a show she'd discuss the script with me, usually at the beginning, but she could always come in at any time." Napier wrote a week or two ahead of recording deadlines, and while tapping out 1,300 episodes of *Portia Faces Life* was a herculean task, his greatest challenge was the soapie *The Guiding Light*, based on American scripts.

"You wouldn't believe how bad some of the American scripts were," lamented Napier. "I mean, *bad*. I'd say to Grace, 'This is hopeless,' and she'd say, 'But that's an *American* script!' She believed there was nothing much to do, just change a few words, and we'd be right. But it was a terrible story and very sloppily put together." In the end, Napier completely rewrote each episode. "We used to do 12 minutes 30 seconds per episode, and the American scripts were running about *seven* minutes. You couldn't possibly work it on what these scripts were, so I got the story content and just started from scratch, and didn't even refer to the American scripts." Napier's scripts ran six foolscap pages for a 12 minutes 30 second episode. He typed the dialogue single-spaced, with a double space between each character's speech. Page count, though, was merely a rough guide to timing. "Eventually you could sense it. Timing was one of those innate things you learned from experience."

Unlike most writers in radio, Napier had a lot of contact with the casts. He was often in the studio doing sound effects. "I was very interested in sound effects … the creeping footsteps coming down the stairs … the fist fights…" He had no formal training, and simply developed the skills by trial and error. Napier sometimes wrote with specific actors in mind. "You'd know their range, what they could do well, but you didn't always have the say. You couldn't tell Lawrie Cecil whom he had to cast — he'd throttle you. I could say to him, 'I think so-and-so might be good', and he'd say, 'yes, that's who I have in mind'. But it could never be your idea — it always had to be Lawrie's. He did the casting, and that was it." Alan White was always Napier's Randy Stone. "He was so good at that first-person narration. He was the best. He was great to write for."

Napier started at £13 a week. And while that was three times the weekly wage that other young men his age received, most freelance radio writers were paid £4 *a script*. Not surprisingly, he eventually went in and asked Grace for a pay rise. According to his calculations, he should have been earning £28 a week.

A steely Grace said, "I want to talk about this. What are your duties each week, Ross? I'd like to put a value on them."

He itemised the number of episodes he wrote each week, and how many shows he did the sound effects for.

"Well, Ross," Grace replied, after consulting her figures, "you're overpaid."

On another occasion, Grace bluntly dismissed his claim for a pay increase. "If I had any choice you wouldn't be here…"

Napier lamented, "She always took the tack that she was subsidising my being there. She wasn't exactly the soul of discretion."

Later, Napier wanted to direct shows, an ambition he shared with panel operator Peter Bernardos. Grace refused point-blank. "You're not going to direct, you're going to stay where you are and write, and Peter isn't going to get anything either." When Napier hinted to Bernardos that he might not have much future with the company, Bernardos said, "Are you trying to get rid of me?"

After four years, Napier resigned. He was a married man and had established himself as one of Australia's leading radio drama writers. It was time to earn some serious money.

"Grace didn't take it kindly when I left. She was bloody furious. She was very harsh. She behaved as though I'd betrayed her." She called Napier all sorts of names, and refused to speak to him on the day he left. "It was a real standoff." Napier left a note on her desk that said, "Thank you for everything … Ross."

Their relationship soured further. Napier freelanced for Grace, finishing off a show called *You Can't Win*, which he had started while he was on staff. The title proved ironically appropriate. "I got them done fairly quickly, put them in, and Grace rang me up and said, 'You wrote those scripts in my time!' I said, 'No, I didn't.' She said, 'You did. You can't write *that fast*.' And she flatly refused to pay me for them."

Meanwhile, Grace berated Reg James in her office. "*Your* friend Ross Napier wrote these scripts in my time!"

Napier took a scriptwriting job with Creswick Jenkinson at Towers of London-Associated Programmes, replacing Peter Yeldham who was going to England. He wrote *Address Unknown* and *Smoky Dawson* for £40 a week. *Address Unknown* was one of Australia's best-loved drama series. Originally created by Jenkinson, it featured documentary-dramas taken "from the files of the Missing Persons Bureau". Napier took over from Yeldham for another 200 episodes, many of which he continued to write when he, too, went to England in 1956.

Happily, the highly quotable closing line of *Address Unknown* could paraphrase Napier's break with Grace — it was "not goodbye, but simply *au revoir*". Back from England, he returned to the Gibson fold, but not on staff. Grace had put the past behind her, if for no other reason than she needed Napier, and if she needed something, business came first.

"I was offered *The Guiding Light*, and then *Cattleman*. But Betty Barnard and I didn't altogether see eye to eye, and she didn't want me to be given *Cattleman*. Grace called me in and told me that Betty didn't want me to have it. Whenever someone said something against a colleague, Grace would always call in that colleague and repeat the accusation."

Cattleman was one of Napier's greatest triumphs. Grace had bought the rights to the novel by R. S. Porteous, which had won a *Courier-Mail* book prize. A family saga set in outback Queensland, it tells how Big Ben McReady carved a life for himself from scratch. As a young cattle duffer, Ben stayed one step ahead of the law; by the time the story has traversed fire, flood and two World Wars, Ben has accumulated riches but his family is divided by greed. Throughout his long life, he is supported by Biddy, an aboriginal girl, whose touching loyalty illuminates the story. Produced in 1961, the serial starred Frank Waters as Ben McReady. Grace sold it as a 208-episode serial, and Ross Napier was stuck with it.

"It was quite a good book, but it wasn't 208 episodes." Napier had to introduce a dynasty of characters; 208 episodes are a lot to get out of a book, and it all had to be dialogue. To make matters worse, the hero's affair with an aboriginal girl, alluded to in the novel, was a particularly thorny issue at that time for country stations. In fact, the worried manager of 2LM Lismore called Reg James to say he had received a complaint about Biddy and thought he should stop playing the serial. While James did not believe in asking listeners for their opinion, on this occasion he suggested it. A few days later the manager rang back happily to say that the show would continue because "everyone loves it".

An even thornier problem for writers like Napier was when characters went missing.

One day in 1963, a listener rang Reg James and asked, "What happened to Portia's daughter?" James put the phone down and scratched his head. Gradually he untangled the real life mystery. Earlier that year, Grace had asked Napier to take over writing *Portia Faces Life* from Coral Lansbury. Lansbury, daughter of Macquarie's sound effects guru Oscar Lansbury, and later the vivacious young widow of George Edwards —

Grace always called her "a Rebecca" — was one of Sydney's most prolific serial writers. A second short marriage saw her become the mother of Liberal Party politician Malcolm Turnbull. Then she announced she was leaving for New Zealand, in pursuit of an academic career and her third husband. Lansbury had been briefed to give Napier a synopsis of the past 100 episodes and an outline of all the characters in the story. She had done that very well, except she overlooked one slight detail: Portia Manning had a daughter. Recalled James, "In one episode of *Portia*, Coral sent the little girl upstairs, and to this day she's still up there because Ross never brought her down."

By the demise of radio drama, Napier was being paid more than any other Gibson writer. "Kath Carroll would have died if she'd have known."

The serials still on air were now being played five mornings a week. Napier was writing a quarter-hour serial called *I, Christopher Macaulay*, and as was the custom, finished it at episode 104. By then, the standard length of a serial had become 130 episodes. Reg James phoned him and asked for another 26 episodes.

Napier had a penchant for unusual titles — *Kinkhead, Goodbye Gwynnevere, Shame of Sefton Ridge, Sinners of Sonoma, Strip Jack Naked* and *Without Shame*. However, to Grace must go the award for the most embarrassing title — *Clayton Place* — which she came up with watching the TV serial *Peyton Place*.

Looking back as a writer, Napier's favourite radio characters were Randy Stone in *Night Beat*, Henry Simon of *Address Unknown*, Ben McReady in *Cattleman*, and the *Castlereagh Line* characters. His association with Gibson's continued until 1986. The only person who worked longer for the company was Reg James.

PETER Yeldham started writing for radio at 17 when he was a messenger boy at 2GB. He used to write scripts at night. "Everyone tried not to tell me how awful they were." The star writers at the station, Richard Lane and Maxwell Dunn, were very helpful. "Finally the script editor accepted one, thinking it would shut me up and I'd go away, but it had the reverse effect." Yeldham had always wanted to be a writer. He went into radio because he couldn't get a job at the *Sydney Morning Herald*. "Rupert Henderson told me I'd have to have a university degree to be a cadet reporter or even a copy boy."

His passion for radio grew. "There was a tremendous amount of production going on. Radio was almost our only local form of entertainment. Movies were all American. We thought in those days we were making the best radio shows in the world, and I sometimes think we were. We made them very quickly." When Yeldham told people he was a writer they used to think, "Oh, you're in the Navy," because a writer was the term for a naval clerk. "There was no prestige in being a writer in those days."

Then Bill Moloney, who wrote a lot of serials for 2UE, asked Yeldham to be his ghost writer while he was away overseas for three months. Yeldham wrote at night and earned extra money so he could take out girls.

Called up in 1945, Yeldham went with the Army as part of the Occupation Force to Japan. He was an announcer and writer with the radio group for 18 months. On his return he was a freelance short story writer living in Kings Cross. "The front door had a letter slot. If you heard a heavy parcel coming through, it was the manuscript coming back. If you heard a little soft noise, it was a cheque."

After breaking into radio with scripts for AWA, he met Grace in 1950 through Betty Barnard. "I think everyone who wanted to work for Grace was offered *Drama of Medicine* because they were 'one-off' quarter-hours. I was a bit in awe of her. She was the top of the tree, as far as I was concerned, but she was very pleasant, easy to talk to." Reg Johnston accepted his first script. "I think I was more in awe of Reg than Grace, because it was Reg who would say yes, we want to use you, or no, we don't. I don't remember how many scripts I wrote when Reg was there, but I was always nervous about how they were going to be received. He had a tremendous reputation, an aura about him. There was a touch of Hollywood about him, a young Zanuck. If you told people you were going to see Reg Johnston, they'd say, 'Oh, how did you get to do that…?'"

Unlike most others, Yeldham called Grace simply Grace. "I don't know why. Probably irreverence…"

The work began to mount up. A *Night Beat* script followed, then *Drama of Medicine* regularly at £3/10/- an episode, which paid the rent. "You had to do quite a lot of writing to make a living. Then I started to write *Medical File*." Next, Yeldham conceived *For the Defence*, dramatised stories about famous defence counsels. "They were largely American or English because in those days there wasn't a great deal of emphasis that we should write about Australia. We all knew New York and London better than we knew Sydney." Mostly he wrote half-hour self-contained dramas for Grace; a notable exception was the successful suspense serial, *The Golden Cobweb*.

He and Grace often discussed scripts. "Grace had a knack of knowing what the market wanted. She liked to say, 'It's going so well so far, what happens next?' and I'd say, 'I don't know until I sit down at the typewriter…' which got her very worried." Yeldham always argued against storylines, plotted well in advance and carved in stone. He once called them, "Those rather plodding and destructive ways to ruin a good story. After that you're just filling in the dots."

By 1953 he was doing more work for Grace than anyone else, and writing a lot for Hilda Scurr at EMI. Yeldham had to write at such speed that it was a long time before he met any actors. He was writing four or five episodes of a serial each week for Grace, as well as two half-hour shows. "I was making about £25 to £30 a week. It was good money, but you really had to work for it. Grace would tell me frequently that I would price myself out of the market. When she had to pay me £25 a week, she paid through gritted teeth."

Yeldham recalls how he always had to see Grace if he wanted a raise. "Val Vine's room had two doors, one into Betty Barnard's office and one into Grace's. I'd arrive and Val would ask if I wanted to see Betty. 'No, I want to see Grace.' Betty was a friend of mine since I was 17, but she was far too tough, she wouldn't give you a brass razoo. Grace would bitch and complain like hell and then say, 'Okay.' Underneath I found her quite soft. Sometimes she'd say 'No, no, you're being paid enough,' and then ring me the next day and say, 'I've been thinking about that, it's okay…' "

On Fridays all the writers went to town to collect their money. "Grace always paid in cash, with a little slip that you signed giving her world rights, but people didn't realise it at the time." With their pockets full of cash, the writers proceeded to the Hotel Australia and got drunk. "It was our watering hole, and we'd all get full as boots — Don Haring, Richard Lane, James Workman, Don Houghton."

There was a lot of true camaraderie amongst the radio writers. "There's none between the writers here in television, it's all dog eat dog, and my return wasn't welcomed with open arms by some people because I seemed to get a lot of the stuff the ABC was doing." But in radio, writers often shared their workload with a mate. "When I was doing a lot of work, *Drama of Medicine* got a bit too much for me. So I said to Don Houghton, who had just arrived and was looking for work, 'Listen, if you ghost a couple of these for me I'll pay you the full fee I'm getting, about £5 an episode, but you mustn't tell Grace because she wouldn't like it.' 'Fine,' Don said. About a week later I got a call from Grace. 'What the hell is this about Don Houghton?' So I said to Don, 'Thanks very much,' and I never saw him again."

In 1954, when he was still in his twenties, Grace asked him to become her production manager. "It sounded a very grand title to me.

We haggled about the money and she offered me £70 a week, which was massive in those days. I was definitely seduced by the money, but I didn't know if I could do the job." John Saul and Lawrie Cecil were directors and I was supposedly in charge of production. I remember once when Ron Randell came back to Australia — by that time he was Ron Ran-*dell* of course — she was showing him round the office. She opened the door and said, 'This is Peter. He might have been a bit young for you to know then,' and Randell said, 'He still looks a bit young…' "

The appointment lasted all of three months and ended in a blazing row with Grace. "I used to work on her scripts at home, a lot at night, and I'd come in late in the morning. If I turned up at ten in the morning, it was anathema to Grace. She wanted me in there at 8.30 if possible, or even 8. In her opinion, I was bludging on the job. I tried to point out what I was doing, and we had a pitched battle in her office. And in the middle of it, Mrs Morgan the tea lady arrived with afternoon tea and had a heart attack. The quarrel stopped and we had to get the tea lady to hospital. I went home and rang Grace that night and said, 'I'm sorry,' and she said, 'No, it's all right, I said a lot of things to you too. I'm having a party on Saturday and I want you to come.' So I said okay, and a lot of the staff were there, like Kath Carroll and a whole lot of others who thought I'd shot my bolt, and when I walked in to Grace's flat their faces were wonderful to behold." In the end, he and Grace decided it was no good him putting on a collar and tie and going to work. "It was not my way, so I went back to being a writer."

As well as Grace's shows, Yeldham wrote *Address Unknown*. "Originally, Peter Finch was going to be the narrator from London, but his fee was too expensive." Instead, actor Lionel Stevens became "Henry Simon". Yeldham also took on scripting *Smoky Dawson*. "Smoky came back from America, and I got conned into writing his show. Why I did it, I suppose, was because Smoky sang a song in every quarter-hour episode so I only had to write nine minutes. I probably wrote eight of those in two days!"

He also adapted Nevil Shute's novel *The Far Country* for EMI. Thirty years later, Hector Crawford assigned him the television adaptation of the same book. "I'd almost forgotten I'd done it for radio until I kept thinking, I know this story very well…"

By 1955 Yeldham decided he was writing too much. He wanted to trade quantity for quality. "I met another writer on the street, Ron Ingleby, who said, 'Oh, I hear you've turned down a show. Are you sick?' And I said, 'No, I just think I'm doing enough.' He looked at me as though I was crazy, because success was measured by the *amount* of work you did, by the yards of words you were writing."

Yeldham went to England in 1956. "I nearly starved for the first couple of years, and then an extraordinary thing happened. Spike Milligan introduced me to his agent, Beryl Vertue."

Vertue worked for a writers' cooperative called Associated London Scripts (ALS), a comedy conglomerate based above a greengrocer's shop in Uxbridge Road. The board of six founding directors — Eric Sykes, Spike Milligan, Ray Galton, Alan Simpson, Frankie Howerd and Scruffy Dale — pooled ten per cent of their incomes to fund what they had conceived as a non-profit-making operation that offered a mutual protection service for writers.

"Beryl was very young, in her early twenties, desperately trying to get on," recalled Yeldham. "She had all these comedy writers, and I was the only drama writer. One morning she rang up to say she'd sold one of my scripts to the BBC. Then an hour later she rang up with news that Granada had bought another script." Another major break came in the form of *Robin Hood*, the British-made TV series starring Richard Greene. Some of the top Hollywood writers, driven out of the States by McCarthyism, worked on it under pseudonyms. Yeldham was assigned an episode. The script paid £1,000.

Yeldham stayed on for twenty years writing plays and series for the BBC and Thames Television, and six West End plays. His credits are awesome. Feature films such as *Age of Consent* with James Mason and Helen Mirren, *The Long Duel* with Yul Brynner, Trevor Howard and Charlotte Rampling, and *The Comedy Man* with Kenneth More; for television, *1915, Run from the Morning, All the Rivers Run, Ride On Stranger,* and *Naked Under Capricorn.* He is now the author of eleven novels such as *A Bitter Harvest* and *The Currency Lads.*

Ironically when his TV plays had to be adapted for radio, he got someone else to do it. "I'd gone so far away from radio. You say everything in radio, and in films you say as little as possible."

WRITERS today can only speculate about the energy and self-discipline required to turn out mountains of radio scripts. Napier and Yeldham typified this dedication to the genre. Both sold their first scripts at 17, both detested the tyranny of storylines plotted in advance, and neither lost their passion.

Napier allocated each day to a different serial; it was impossible to jump from one show to another in the same day. "It was too hard, you'd get mixed up." He got up at 5 a.m., and went for a walk. If he was doing a book adaptation he read a chapter, put the book away, and did not leave his typewriter that day until he was finished. On average, each page of script took ten minutes to write.

Yeldham, too, planned his writing time meticulously. When he wrote a "one-off" that needed a self-contained story, Yeldham and his wife Marge sat up at night and worked out the plot. Next morning he started writing at 5 a.m., aiming to finish a quarter of it before a late breakfast at nine. He then wrote on and finished by four that afternoon. Quarter-hour serials demanded an equally rigorous schedule; Yeldham wrote four episodes a day so he could keep track of the plot and all the loose threads. One episode had to be completed before breakfast, two in the afternoon, and the fourth before the next morning. "The early start was very important in those days. I couldn't do it now and I don't know how I did it then."

Weekends were sacrosanct. "We never worked on weekends. In those days, shops shut at twelve o'clock on Saturday and didn't open again until Monday. We were like that with our typewriters."

In terms of craft, Napier and Yeldham shared many similarities.

Both found timing was an innate, intuitive skill, the product of experience — six or seven pages of foolscap, with Grace insisting on single-spacing between speeches to save paper. And both treasured the liberation of controlling the story as it happened. Sometimes Napier had a rough plot in mind, "but I preferred to write as it came, because it was more entertaining for me. I think I would have died of boredom if I'd known where all these things were actually going. In *Castlereagh Line*, when Gordon died, I didn't have the least idea of killing him. But right at the end of an episode he'd gone to the door and opened it, and I went 'Bang!' and wrote down 'Pistol shot, reaction, music to end'. And I thought when I'd done it, my God, that'll knock them!" When Napier told the actor what he'd done, he wasn't too happy; but such was the power of the scriptwriter.

FOR serious actors like Michael Pate, the script was not a means to an end; it was the beginning of a journey. He always collected his scripts before the actual recording. "I used to live in Neutral Bay in those days and I'd get the ferry. The whole 20 minutes on the ferry would be spent reading the scripts. When I got home I'd start marking the scripts — all my speeches, and the emphases underneath my lines, and I'd use different coloured pencils. I'd put question marks on things to ask the producer — what does this line mean? There was an enormous amount of work preparing those scripts."

Some writers peppered their scripts with instructions for the cast. "Most of the better writers in those days, to the best of my remembrance, didn't put a lot of that in," Pate observed. "If it were very necessary, if it wasn't obvious in the script that he would laugh, you would be asked to do that. It might say, 'he cackles' or 'he sneers'. But we worked at that ourselves, and we felt that we had a lot of liberty to put those things in ourselves. If we wanted to laugh, we would. We did whatever the character would do. We were given the liberty to do a lot of things like that, which were part of the character. And we did a lot of constructed things. We would sometimes shape scripts that we were in, add words to them, or take words out to make them better."

Pate believed the quality of the writing in general was very good. "A lot of it was adaptations, *Bishop's Mantle* was adapted, *Escape Me Never* was adapted, and there were any number of things that I did with Eric Scott that were adaptations of Dumas, Senior and Junior — *Man In the Iron Mask, Count of Monte Cristo, The Three Musketeers*. They were all quality things, the dialogue was there, and you weren't going to fool around with Dumas or Balzac or Daphne du Maurier. There was the other kind of stuff that sometimes was knocked out, just as it's knocked out today. Some of the language was a little poor. Once or twice you'd pick up an illiterate script. So you'd make your little remarks and you'd go in early and talk to the producer. But there was a terrible inclination to say, 'Oh well, that's good enough', and that came in after I went to America."

BY the late 1950s, the fee for a quarter-hour script was around £5. Residuals were non-existent. Writers had to turn out at least ten scripts a week to make a living. Some managed more. They were a lonely, hard-drinking bunch. Many suffered breakdowns.

Sadly, scripts were all too often churned out, arguably to the detriment of the industry. Some of Grace's shows bore all the evidence of slipshod writing. As far as Reg James was concerned, *All This and Heaven Too* didn't even make sense. "The scripts were based on Rachel Field's novel. I went in to John Saul and said, 'John, I don't understand this show.' 'I know,' replied Saul, 'but I'm not worried. I just get the scripts, and I go in there and produce them.' We'd sold the show to the Major network, and when it came back we never offered it for sale again."

In 1940, E. Mason Wood had created one of radio's most enduring characters, *Doctor Mac*, brought to life by Lou Vernon. It ran for 11 years. But *Doctor Mac*, which played on 2GB, and 2UE's top-rating *Officer Crosby* were being written by the same man, Billy Moloney. The former was about a warm, homespun Scottish family doctor; the latter about a warm, homespun family policeman. According to popular legend at the time, Moloney used the same scripts and simply changed the character's names. Coral Lansbury was rumoured to have done something similar when she wrote *The Reverend Matthew* for Grace. At the same time she was writing a serial about a doctor for ABC. Both characters and stories were interchangeable.

At the very least, knowing Grace's fanaticism about scripts, her writers kept to their deadlines.

Usually the scripts were handed in well ahead of recording deadlines, and there was time to go through them and make changes. Occasionally the situation got precarious, and the main culprit, recalled James, was actor-turned-writer Harp McGuire.

"It was a rarity to type scripts straight onto stencils and it should never have happened. When Harp was writing *The Saga of Davy Crockett*, which was pretty crook, we were recording ten episodes a day. Five in the morning and five in the afternoon, and he'd be writing the ones for the afternoon during the lunch hour." The Fess Parker movie had started the Davy Crockett craze in the 1950s, and 2UE, 2UW's Fidelity and Grace Gibson each produced a Davy Crockett serial. Other problems dogged the show. McGuire acted in the serial with Canadian Joe McCormack. One day, they kept fluffing their lines, and one master after another was trashed. Finally, engineer John Woodward lost his genial composure and bawled them out in the studio.

Another offender was Lindsay Hardy. James had instructions not to let him out of his office until he had finished writing. "He was dreadful.

I'd stand at the door and he couldn't come out. On a Friday, we'd go up to the Carlton or the Metropole looking for him." Despite Hardy's unpredictability his standard never dropped. Yet, as time went by, observed James, he seemed trapped in a Gregory Keen time warp. "When he went to England and the United States, he recycled his old radio concepts. He sold *Dossier on Dumetrius* as a film, then most of his others he sold to the BBC and he wrote the scripts. *Walk a Crooked Mile* became *A Mask for Alexis*. When he did the basic scripting for a 1963 movie called *Love is a Ball*, which starred Charles Boyer and Glenn Ford, it was based on his comedy adventure serial called *The Knave of Hearts*. *Stranger in Paradise* was published in an American magazine as *Morning After Murder*, and *Twenty-Six Hours* as *The Faceless Ones*. It also appears he wrote other stories for television and magazines. His Gregory Keen stories were translated into about ten different languages."

AS THE 1950s progressed, there was no time for the passion and quality demanded by men like Reg Johnston, or the punctilious professionalism of Michael Pate. The days of the early perfectionists were over. If radio drama was headed for oblivion, then every minute might be its last — or so it seemed. The industry worked at a frenzied pace.

For some studios, harried writers hammered their scripts straight on to stencils, beating deadlines with only minutes to spare. It was the norm.

Stencils arrived moments before the actors did. Pages came off the duplicating machine as the episode was being recorded. There was no time for them to dry, so they were passed straight through into the studio — covered with wet ink! Dinah Shearing was recording at George Edwards's studio and had been told she would be playing two parts. When a fresh, wet, inky page was suddenly handed to her, she realised that two speeches further on she would be playing a scene with herself — as a young woman about her own age, with the other character being an older woman. While the great George Edwards could play dozens of different voices, Shearing was still very young and inexperienced. She was terrified, but did the scene. "I *had to!*" To separate the two voices, Shearing made the older woman *exceptionally* old.

Alastair Duncan still shudders at memories of *The Air Adventures of Biggles*. "At AWA with Col Craigen doing *Biggles*, the scripts were handed to you in the studio, page by wet page, and whoever was doing the writing had not a great idea of timing. So Craigen would be signalling mighty stretches, and whoever was playing Biggles would say, 'Yes, well I decided to go to the store because we need a few groceries, and I bought half a pound of bacon and a dozen eggs.' And the other fellow would say, 'Oh, did you? And what else did you get?' 'Yes, well, it was quite an interesting shop and I met one or two people I knew actually, but we did need some stores for the next flight…' And sometimes there would be three or four minutes of it being ad-libbed. It was absolutely incredible."

Peter Yeldham called it a frightening experience. "Some writers were doing so much they'd actually bring in their scripts on stencils, and they'd be run off and rushed straight in to the actors. I was actually directing a show like that, which Richard Lane wrote. You'd start with two scripts, and Dick would be somewhere in Sydney writing the rest, and ferrying the stencils into the studio by taxi."

There was no time for research. Nor could writers rely on experts such as lawyers or doctors to vet their scripts. Grace was sued once over an episode in the *Drama of Medicine* about a Chinese doctor, a hero during the Second World War. "Unbeknown to us the doctor survived the war and went to live in New Zealand where he heard the programme. He wasn't amused. Or maybe he just didn't like the accent we gave him," speculated Reg James. "It was settled very quickly."

When television arrived, a lot of writers tried to equate what they were paid to write radio scripts with what they were paid to write TV scripts. "They believed they weren't being paid enough for radio," said James. "I remember one writer telling me, 'Well, I can only afford to spend an hour writing this episode.' And he tried to do that. It never worked. Some episodes you *could* breeze through, but not all. The awful part was, this writer wasn't getting any television writing."

COMEDY was Grace's least successful genre. While she was recognized as the English-speaking world's most successful exponent of long running dramatic serials, comedy remained elusive.

In the early 1950s she recorded local versions of top US radio comedy shows *Fibber McGee and Molly* and *My Friend Irma*. They were financially successful, received no criticism, but were never classed as "hits". In 1970, while Grace was in Honolulu, Ross Napier had the concept for a 3-minute self-contained comedy feature called *No, Mrs Maddox*. Reg James approved the idea and auditions were recorded starring Gordon Chater and Ruth Cracknell. The 130 episodes were sold without difficulty but were not overly popular with audiences. It was a boisterous show, and told of a noisy woman's attempt to obtain a driver's licence. On her return, Grace was not amused.

AS RADIO drama matured and entered its final phase, narration fell into disrepute. The narrated top and tail of an episode was one of radio's oldest conventions. "In our last episode…" began each new one, launching into a summary of the story thus far. And with the cliffhanger ending came the narrator's familiar exhortation: "Stay tuned for the next exciting episode…"

But was narration nothing more than lazy writing — the scriptwriter taking the easy way out?

The opening narration from an American script, *Till the Day I Die*, typified radio dramas of the 1940s. The play was probably the last radio show recorded by Peter Finch before he left for the UK:

NARR: Picture an ordinary hotel room. The breeze comes gently through a window, flapping at the blind. Below in the street the traffic passes noisily by, unheeded by the young man who sits by the window looking fixedly toward the sky. He stubs his cigarette into an already crammed ashtray. His gaunt face is drawn, his mind reeling with a thousand confused thoughts.

Narration from *The Shadow* demonstrated how the radio writer could remind listeners of the key characters while establishing a new story:

NARR: The Shadow, who aids the forces of law and order, is in reality Lamont Cranston, wealthy young man-about-town. Years ago in the Orient, Cranston learned a strange and mysterious secret — the hypnotic power to cloud men's minds so they cannot see him. Cranston's friend and companion, the lovely Margo Lane, is the only person who knows to whom the voice of the invisible Shadow belongs.
  (PAUSE)
Today's drama – Spotlight on the Duchess.
C.O. ORGAN THEME. FADE FOR …
  NARR: (CUE) The scene is set in a low-class saloon, filled with the wispy haze of cigarette smoke. On a high stool, leaning against the counter, is a blousy, peroxided blonde, her heavily lined face streaked with thickly caked make-up…

Narration, said Napier, often got out of hand. "Long narrations were common in the old days. But if you've got a narration telling the damn story you don't need actors." Instead, Napier changed its form: the characters themselves replaced the traditional narrator. "The characters told the story. You could have two or three characters all telling the story from different angles which was very effective at getting the story over."

Yeldham believed narration had its place. "If it was an historical thing like *Famous Trials*, you had to narrate to tell people where you were. Serials needed narration, too, even if it was a character in the serial, just to say what was happening."

One Sydney producer, Gordon Grimsdale, did not accept any scripts with narration.

By the 1960s, such discussions had largely become academic.

THOSE plays, and those days, will never come again.

American writer Brock Bower observed: "Nothing like them will ever be done on television because they demand the very thing TV has scotched: imagination."

Or, as Stan Freberg put it, television stretched the imagination — up to 21 inches.

Episode 9

Next stop, Hollywood

"YOU just knew that Peter Finch was going to be a star."

Grace's instinct for talent was unswervingly accurate. Finch starred in many early shows. He was in the first episode of *The Shadow*, and a Caltex Star Theatre drama called *Till the Day I Die*.

"I knew Peter personally quite well," she confided many years later. "I always knew Peter would go places because he was an artist. He was very sincere about his acting, and he was sincere about his drinking, too. He liked the girls, he was great fun, and he was really a bad boy, but deep down in his heart he was very sincere about his acting and you couldn't take that away from him."

Finch was always hard to book. He never had an agent, and didn't answer phone calls. Finch thought radio serials were fun at first, then he became ashamed of them. He had won Macquarie Awards for radio acting two years running, 1946 and 1947. But there was no place for serious acting; Australia was a theatrical desert. It was fluffy operettas at J. C. Williamson's, or radio serials. He founded the Mercury Theatre with John Kay, a classical repertory theatre, financed by their earnings from the Mercury acting school. Later they toured factories performing Molière. It was at a lunchtime show at the O'Brien glass factory that Sir Laurence Olivier and Vivien Leigh discovered him in August 1948. By November, Finch was in London.

Peter Yeldham knew him slightly. "I was in a pub when he came in one day and announced he was going to England, and that Laurence Olivier and Vivien Leigh were going to look after him. He went around the pub borrowing money for his fare. I gave him a quid, which was all I could afford at the time."

Michael Pate hailed Finch as one of the best radio actors. "Finchie did quite a lot of work before the war with the ABC, and when he came back he did a little bit more work, but he pursued the Mercury Theatre. Then he took Molière out to the factories and caught Larry Olivier's attention in 1948 when the Old Vic came out. From then he was out of the picture as far as I remember. I never cared for him in everything he did on the stage, I thought he was a bit too contrived, but on radio he was absolutely incredible. He had the most wonderful, wonderful voice. It was the same when he was first in films in England. He was lousy in films when he first appeared, and look at what a wonderful, wonderful actor he became."

RON Randell had been the first to go to Hollywood. Randell had compered Grace's first show, *Here Are the Facts*, in 1944. He starred as Australian aviator Sir Charles Kingsford-Smith in Columbia's *Smithy*, then appeared with Ginger Rogers and Cornel Wilde in *It Had to Be You*.

Randell and Kitty Bluett had been an item in post-War Sydney entertainment. They drove around together in an open tourer.

In 1949, the 31-year-old Randell moved to America permanently, working in films, TV and stage plays. Randell became Ran-*dell*. Described by the British cinema author Leslie Halliwell as an "Australian leading man with radio experience", Randell's screen credits rapidly accumulated: *Lorna Doone* (1950), *Kiss Me Kate* with Howard Keel, Kathryn Grayson and Ann Miller (1953), two Bulldog Drummond flicks, *I Am a Camera* (1955), *The Story of Esther Costello* (1958), *King of Kings* (1961), and Darryl F. Zanuck's *The Longest Day* (1962).

Two decades later he co-starred with Richard Gere in the Broadway premiere of *Bent*, a play depicting the persecution of homosexuals in Nazi Germany.

MICHAEL Pate was one of the leading men that Grace most adored. Talking about his Hollywood success she would say: "Michael could play Red Indians, but there was no disguising his beautiful voice. He played the lead in a show called *The Bishop's Mantle* for us. It was a lovely show."

Pate had been discharged from the Army in 1946 and gone filming all of 1947 in *Sons of Matthew* at £25 a week. Then extra shots were needed and the production dragged on until March 1948. "By that time, it was known as *Grandsons of Matthew!* I came back to Sydney and I was looking for work. The radio work was our constant work. I went to see Edward Howell at AWA, and Reg Johnston, Betty Barnard and the girls at Grace Gibson. We had nerves of steel and stomachs of cast iron because all that stuff in those days went down onto wax discs. Grace set a very high standard for herself. She was a practical, down-to-earth person. A lot of people thought she was a bit brash, a bit Yankee, but she really was a very smart cookie. Grace was always immaculately dressed, her hair coiffed. She was always available in her office if you wanted to go up and say hello. And she was always nice."

Pate starred in two of Grace's early successes: *The Bishop's Mantle* with Sheila Sewell in 1948, when he was 28, and *Escape Me Never* with Marion Johns in 1949.

"In those days you had to be of a very high standard before you got work. Anybody that fooled around, or was drunk or otherwise, was *persona non grata*. Radio established a kind of discipline for us, and a kind of perfection in our work that went around the world. The thing was, we were in a group of people whose standard was so high, that we could not afford to be less than that high standard. They were all so skilled, they could all do lots of accents, they recorded tens of hundreds of shows a year. We vied with each other to be perfect — that's why we did so much work in those days. When you looked at the talent that was around — Johnnie Saul, Georgie Sterling, Bettie Dickson, Brenda Dunrich, and Reg Johnston, a marvellous director."

Pate started off at £1/2/10 an episode. "But we all gradually said, 'Grace, I'm playing the lead, what's it worth?' And so all of our prices went up. I finished up getting, for some shows, three or four guineas a performance. We had always got three or four guineas a performance at the ABC back in 1938!"

Pate was firmly established as a radio star, one of the reigning giants of the local Hollywood. "Being a radio star then was like being a movie star today. People knew you, you got written about in the magazines like the *Listener-In*, the *ABC Weekly*. People nudged each other and whispered when they passed a radio star in the street. We were just so much part of their lives."

His own mother was no exception. When he was doing *The Bishop's Mantle*, and Thelma Scott was playing the seductress, his mother went up to the public phone box on the corner and rang him.

She rarely made phone calls and Pate was immediately concerned. "What is it?" he asked her. "Something wrong?"

"I'm a bit worried."

"Yes?"

"You know that *Bishop's Mantle*," she said, "I'm very worried about that other woman in it…"

Pate had to carefully reassure her. "She really believed that we were those people and you were hearing it over radio. She just couldn't visualise me in a studio doing a play. She thought that this was actually happening between us all, and she was able to hear it."

Pate himself was a product of Drummoyne Primary School, ostensibly one of the places least likely to produce a great actor. Not that Pate had ever aspired to act. "I had one thought when I was growing up. I wanted to be a medical missionary."

Grace was not the first to recognise Pate's fine voice, and on that score Drummoyne can take a bow. "I never had a voice lesson in my life. Singing in choirs helped me; you have to be able to stand properly, you must be able to breathe properly. I had an almost two-octave range. At school we spoke poetry in class. Without knowing it, we were being taught how to open our voices up. At one time I could have quoted a great deal of *Hamlet*, and all of *Richard III*, all of *Romeo and Juliet*, and most of *Macbeth*, speech after speech after speech. We knew them, we learned them." Sitting in the local cinema, Pate absorbed the cadences and clarity of Ronald Colman and Robert Donat. "Their voices were beautiful and the recording was always very good." Pate and his contemporaries exercised their voices. "If someone was having a problem we'd say take the telephone book, read it and make it interesting for us. And you could. You could really use your voice." A singer once told him: "Try whistling. You'll find that will give you the mouth formations." Today, it's a different story for young actors. "They all sound very similar, all the girls sound alike, all the boys sound alike. It's not because they aren't individually shaped; after all, we all have our own throats, and diaphragms, and we are all different. I think it's because they're drenched so much with what is average in standard. Everything has become so homogenised that everyone has become homogenised on the screen as well. But when I started acting, the material was very diverse, we did all kinds of plays, and we had to be adaptable, no matter what medium we worked in, and use our voices."

Diversity bred versatility. Actors needed a bank of character voices and accents, and had to be ready to deploy them on everything from classical ABC plays to soap operas. "We were vocal chameleons, and we were probably Machiavellians into the bargain. We saw a lot of movies in those days, people with French accents, Spanish accents, and Linguaphone had an album with two dozen accents of the British Isles." Pate even tracked down people of the required nationality; while they read the script to him, he wrote out the part phonetically. Once he had to play a Viennese count. His father-in-law at the time was a Hungarian who spoke German. Pate felt it would have been an imposition if he asked for help outright. Instead, he saw him fairly regularly, and afterwards jotted down words from their conversations, carefully analysing the old man's cadences. Pate told him to listen to the play, and his father-in-law reported back: "Michael, it was a wonderful play, the way you talked I could believe you were in Vienna. It was marvellous, it reminded me of somebody I know…"

Pate's attention to his wardrobe was as meticulous as his working methods. "We didn't have that many things. Nigel Lovell always dressed well, so did Max Osbiston, and we shopped very well. If we went to a department store very early on a Friday morning we'd find they'd have quite a few bargains. And if those didn't suit us, we'd go around and change the price tags on things that did. Why not? They had more money than we did."

Fortunately for the retailers, Pate's income rapidly increased. "Before the War, I probably made eight or ten or twelve guineas a week. I lived on a couple of quid a week, and my room cost me six and six a week." In post-War radio, his earnings doubled. "£25 a week was good money in those days. I picked up my scripts on Friday night for the next week, and I always carried a brief case, it was always full of scripts. I was doing a couple of one-hour shows plus 20 quarter-hours in a week, and I might be reading something for the ABC."

By the time he left for Hollywood, Pate was earning £65 a week. "That was gigantic. I was getting a few extra quid for doing a *Lux Radio Theatre*. I started Lux on about £12, then I went to £20, and then I went to £25, something like that." Before he left he had to finish recording a serial for George Edwards, and recorded 14 half-hour scripts over two mornings.

Pate had always wanted to go to America. When he got there, he was horrified to discover how fast Australians actually spoke. He was called to the studio to loop [post-synch] some scenes in his first film, *Thunder on the Hill*. After several attempts had failed to synchronise his new speech with his lip movements on the screen, he turned to the projectionist and said, "Your projector seems to be running too fast." The technician said, "No, Mike, it's running at 24 frames. It's just that you were speaking faster when you filmed the scene."

Soon, Pate found himself as busy as ever. Stirling Macoboy, the executive producer of the *Lux Radio Theatre* in Australia, had contacted his counterparts in Hollywood. "I did a dozen *Lux Radio Theatres* in Hollywood — the first was with Jimmy Stewart and Marlene Dietrich, the second with Stewart Granger and Deborah Kerr. Meanwhile, he went from one film to another — a movie with James Mason, *Five Fingers*, then a film with Charles Laughton, "and it just went on from there".

ANOTHER young actor whose career Grace nurtured was Rod Taylor. "He was a different kettle of fish to Peter Finch," she pointed out. "I knew him just as well as Peter, and he took his acting seriously."

When Taylor first appeared in shows like *Night Beat* in 1950, he was a dedicated, dashingly handsome art student with a devastating effect on women. In one of his earliest serials for Grace, *The Strange Life of Deacon Brodie*, he was billed in the credits as "Rodney Taylor".

Despite his gift for drama, Taylor was always oddly nervous in the studio. Her producer, John Saul, became Taylor's guru. Their friendship endured, and Saul and his wife Georgie Sterling would be Taylor's frequent houseguests in Hollywood.

When Taylor's performances won him an overseas trip in 2UE's Actor's Choice competition, he opted for Hollywood.

Within six years of his debut as a raw amateur in Sydney radio, he was appearing with namesake Elizabeth Taylor in two major movies

— *Giant* and *Raintree County*. In 1960 he was a star in his own right in *The Time Machine*, based on the H. G. Wells novel. Television brought him to the attention of worldwide audiences as the star of the adventure series, *Hong Kong*. His greatest achievements came in 1963: the starring role in the Alfred Hitchcock classic, *The Birds*, followed by *The VIPs* with Elizabeth Taylor and Richard Burton.

CHARLES "Bud" Tingwell was another of the "Gibson boys" who stepped from behind the microphone to find fame and fortune overseas. In fact, Grace was the first to recognise his film and television potential when she cast him as the star in the pilot episode of a proposed TV drama series.

Tingwell chose the traditional route to London where he became one of the first stars of British television in the series *Emergency Ward Ten*. His movie credits included *Murder She Said,* playing the harried police inspector opposite the endearing Margaret Rutherford in the role of Agatha Christie's Miss Marple.

OTHER radio stars never made it overseas. In one tragic incident in 1957, Lloyd Berrell set out for London but died at the age of 32 on board the ship that was taking him there. One rumour suggested that he died of malnutrition because his diet consisted of meat pies. ("Malnutrition?" queried a friend. "I wouldn't have thought so.") Given Berrell's talent, there is every likelihood he would have carved out a career in the UK.

The same could be said for June Salter, who had honed her skills in many of Grace's serials. Except Salter didn't make it, ironically through no fault of her own. She was offered a major role in one of Peter Yeldham's BBC TV plays. But it wasn't to be. Her husband John Meillon refused to babysit their child for the three or four days she would be working in Manchester. For Salter, opportunity only knocked once. Soon she returned home. Meillon came too, also forfeiting the chance of a big career.

ABSENCE makes the heart grow fonder, and for Australian actors working in London this was particularly true. Had theirs been a love-hate relationship with Grace, or had there perhaps been more love?

One morning after Peter Yeldham had established himself in London, he received a phone call. Grace and Ronnie were in town and wanted to see him. Yeldham decided to organise a big party for them.

It was like a huge, latter day casting call for all the expatriate Australian actors who had ever worked on her shows back home. Wherever Grace turned, familiar faces beamed back. She greeted Alan White like a long-lost son. Yeldham recalled, "I rang up thirty, forty people. Not one of them said 'no'. They all said they'd love to see the old girl. It was a very merry evening."

Episode 10

The one-eyed monster

THE first television stations went to air in 1956. Suddenly, crowds were clamouring outside electrical stores, spellbound by the crude blue images flickering on the screens of Admiral TV sets.

Television was a reality, yet many in radio confidently predicted the survival of the big national shows. And survive they did, for another four years. In fact, in 1958 export sales of Australian radio dramas were worth over US$1.25 million a year. Yet within six years countless thousands of episodes of old radio shows were sold off and melted down as aggregate for new expressways.

IT WERE as though television was still light years away. Grace's fifth iconic long run soapie went to air on 2UW starting 18 August 1959.

The Guiding Light, reproduced from American television scripts sponsored by Procter & Gamble on the NBC Network, would run for 1,040 episodes. Grace's programme blurb stated:

> This serial has won many thousands of devoted friends as a "different" serial ... a serial with inspirational appeal for all who are ready to receive its philosophical, spiritual and religious message. It is the story of the Reverend Thomas Andrews ... the Good Samaritan who possesses a human warmth and down-to-earth charm.

Clearly, clerics provided good copy for Grace's serial mill.

DESPITE the industry's buoyant mood, Grace, who had presided over radio drama all her life, heard the bell tolling. The order went out: "We tighten up our shows, make them move faster, and do away with narration as much as possible."

And, long before television reached Australia, Grace had decided to stake a claim in the new medium.

"THERE'S a difference between a man that has a licence and a man that wants a licence," said Grace.

The man in question was her old friend and mentor, Sir Frank Packer.

Before TV was introduced into Australia, Packer was after a licence. As Grace confided, "He'd never even owned a radio station so I used to go up to his office and help him as much as I could regarding his application for a television licence. I had lots of pilot films sent out from America for him to view."

With typical foresight, Grace planned to represent Hollywood programme makers in much the same way she had represented the old radio transcription houses. At one stage she even secured the Australian rights to *I Love Lucy*, and foreshadowed Reg Grundy by conceptualising audience participation shows and panel discussions. And the plan might have worked. However, once he was awarded the television licence for Channel 9 Sydney, Packer decided to buy programmes direct from their source in Hollywood. Grace was out.

She felt betrayed by her old friend. As Ross Napier recalled, "She was going to do all sorts of things, and she probably would have, but I think that Frank Packer thing put a torpedo in her bows."

AWARE of television's impact on American radio drama, Grace had also embarked on her most ambitious project: Sunset Film Promotions.

She'd done her homework. "I didn't think you could get your money back, and you certainly couldn't in those days, by producing shows for just Australia." So Grace set her sights on America.

In the early 1950s, American TV stations were spending over US$300 million a year on programme production. Larger American cities could already boast 13 channels, many transmitting 24 hours a day. Colour television was just around the corner. It was scheduled to launch on New Year's Day, 1954, and the first sets would cost US$800 each.

Grace was determined to produce a TV show in Australia that was good enough to sell overseas. The company was set up to make three-reel, thirty-minute TV films with Australian stars, producing them cheaply enough to gain a foothold in the American market. She got together with three American friends and they put up the capital.

The first pilot was *I Found Joe Barton*, starring Charles Tingwell, Margo Lee and Lloyd Berrell, shot in 1952. It told the story of an American film magnate who made a movie about an American criminal, only to learn that he was still alive and living in Sydney. Ex-G.I. Al Munch, played by Tingwell, is hired to track him down and buy his silence. Grace imported an American director, Francis D. (Pete) Lyon, who had won an Academy Award for the editing of the John Garfield boxing film, *Body and Soul*. The *ABC Weekly* hailed the pilot show as "first-rate", praised its "crispness and compactness", and congratulated Grace for trying to give Australian talent a stand. Tingwell, said the reviewer with foresight, "is probably Australia's best film bet."

Grace had never worked harder. She was starting her television production venture while taking over British Australian Programmes. Sadly, the television venture failed.

"We had a screening of it one night for the people who were interested in television licences and they all thought it was wonderful. It was too early for them to buy it for Australia because the licences hadn't been granted yet. So we sold it to MCA, one of America's biggest production companies. They owned Universal Studios and I had quite a few dealings with the president, Lou Wassermann. They paid us peanuts for it. They said they would have bought the entire series if we produced the 13 episodes first, but the cost was so damned high that we didn't go through with it." Making that one episode had set Grace back £10,000.

Joe Barton was aired in America once, sponsored by a soft drink company, and released in Australia through Greater Union Theatres. It also saw the light of day in Pakistan, Sri Lanka, Burma and India.

Her staff wanted her to go into television, but Grace was adamant. "I've made my money, and I'm not going to lose it trying to do television programmes." Years later she came to regret that decision. "I think that we could have done with television what we did with radio…"

That challenge would be left in the hands of her old radio competitors, Hector and Dorothy Crawford.

BY 1960, radio drama was well into its sunset years. The medium was redefining itself. *Night Beat* was replaced by a different beat. The DJs were taking over from the dramas. For Grace and her staff it was a painful time. One blow followed another.

"Every year the Major Network held a conference deciding on programme purchases, and we spent a lot of time making audition programmes to present to them," said Reg James. "It was a bit scary because we needed them to buy nationally. In 1962, they purchased a number of new quarter-hour serials including *I Know My Love*, based on a Catherine Gaskin romance set in the Victorian Gold Rush. It was a network sale except Victoria, for £34 an episode payable six-monthly. It started on 2UE on 19 November 1962, four episodes a week, Monday to Thursday."

Within a matter of weeks, 2UE, a bastion of radio drama for thirty years, announced it was putting its morning serials away for the Christmas holidays.

They were never heard again.

Episode 11

The long good-bye

RADIO drama did not die overnight; rather, it was a long, slow fade-out. For a while in the late 1950s, sales actually boomed. Overseas exports reached a record high. Meanwhile at home, not all markets had television; sales of drama to metropolitan and country stations continued, creating an illusion of false security. As Reg James reflected: "We just put TV out of our minds and went on. And we succeeded, because we went on producing radio drama for a long time."

Inexorably though, TV audiences grew and sponsors switched to the new medium. The big radio networks gradually shrank in power and prestige. The old radio theatres were boarded up, dismantled or demolished.

Night Beat ceased production in the middle of 1959. The sponsor, James Stedman Henderson, wanted to put its money into TV advertising. It purchased repeat performances for another two years for those stations in rural markets that had no TV coverage. Other stations, including 2GB, purchased their own repeat performances so Randy Stone continued to be heard well into the late 1960s.

By then, the bubble of the late-50s boom had burst.

ROSS Napier and his wife Ann Fuller packed their bags and headed for London in 1956. "I left a couple of the best years of radio behind.

I went to England to get TV experience. We all had a feeling that TV was coming, but I didn't think it was going to do what it did. It wiped out radio serials virtually overnight. Suddenly it was all over. The actors were talking about it in the studio — television's coming to gobble us all up."

Peter Yeldham also saw the writing on the wall. "The authorities were holding an open inquiry into television in 1955. I went along and Frank Packer was on the stand. Twenty people were there. Clive Evatt from Actors Equity asked him, 'Will you agree to a quota, Mr Packer?' And he said, 'No, but Australians know me. I'll treat them the way I've always treated them.' When I heard that, I went straight home and said, 'Let's go to England!'"

Another disconcerting factor was the production of the American TV series *Long John Silver* in Sydney. Yeldham and other Australian writers had called up and offered to contribute scripts to the series. The Americans said, "No, we don't want any Australian scripts." They'd brought their own scripts, director and key crew, and it was a bitter taste of the future.

When Yeldham told Grace about his impending departure, she said, "Don't go to England, I've been there, it's lousy." Then she gave Yeldham's wife Marge 208 episodes of *Girl from Nowhere* to adapt, which meant just taking out the Americanisms, to help pay for the trip.

Like Napier, Yeldham had not expected radio drama to vanish so quickly. "I didn't actually realise it would end quite the way it did." He was in England when the serials were being taken off air. "I didn't hear about it all at once, just gradually as people came over. It was sad, it was like the whole industry just ceased to exist, and for a long time it wasn't replaced by anything until Hector Crawford." Radio had been his passion and within a decade it had vanished. "I think I would have been devastated if I'd been in Australia..."

One writer committed suicide. A lot of the actors were out of work.

Some of Napier's childhood acting heroes resorted to driving cabs for a living.

John Woodward had been part of the young, pioneering radio generation of the 1930s. Now he watched as the medium contracted from big shows to news-and-music formats. "I'd handled *Fred and Maggie Everybody* with old Ted Howell and Therese Desmond. And one of the things we did at AWA every year was the Humphrey Bishop pantomime, in the big studio originally up at the Grace Building. When the AWA Building was built, we did it up there. He even had these curtains with 'HB' on them, a full orchestra and singers. But when TV hit the scene, there was an economic recession in the recording industry. It was a whole different ball game."

When TV started, Reg James was 27. He had spent the first ten years of his working life with Grace and now it seemed the industry was finished. Radio drama was hardly a smart career choice for a young man. "But I never thought of going into TV," he confessed. "I just thought, Grace will survive. I had implicit faith in her." Like Woodward, James could profess a love of radio. He had started listening to it in the early 1930s, and the shows, the stories, the voices had become part of him. Radio drama was in his blood. The same could be said for Ross Napier. "He never really got away from it," said James.

APART from the coming of television, many believed that the radio stations and production companies themselves sped the demise of radio drama.

"Shows were played on so many stations, for such long periods, that we could not really keep up the supply, and stations would buy almost anything." Reg James remembered how shows such as *Dr Paul* suffered because stations had commenced broadcasting news on the hour. "The three minutes of news ate into the broadcast of a 15-minute serial. The panel operator would just drop the needle onto the record sometime during the opening narration. Nobody seemed to care."

NOBODY seemed to care.

Most radio production companies still "flew" episodes without rehearsal and actors coasted through their formulaic scripts.

Michael Pate made a brief visit to Sydney in 1959. He called in to see Reg Southey at EMI, which had then moved to Castlereagh Street. "They were recording some stuff, and I was up in the control room with Reg, and I'd been listening to it. It was so undisciplined, they were all 'codding' it up, a terrible standard of acting, it was lousy, and it sounded terrible. And I said to Reg, 'God, I've only been away ten years, what's happened? When I was here you wouldn't have worked again if you fooled around like that…' And Reg said, 'Ah, yes, but you see, you're not here,' and he went through the whole bloody list of all the people we used to work with, like Nancye Stewart and Lou Vernon. Those actors we worked with were all old pro's, they didn't fool around, they came in to work, and they got paid good money for it, and they instilled in all us young ones that you didn't fool around in the profession, the profession meant too much. When I got back and was watching that session at EMI, and they were all fooling around, and galah-ing, I thought, God almighty, thank God I don't have to do that again, that would've made me very disturbed."

It wasn't just the acting that shocked Pate. "The writing had slipped, it was soap opera rubbish they were writing. When I got scripts that weren't good — and I did this in Hollywood when I was working there, I did 350 scripts over there — I would sit down and work at it, and I'd go in and make an appointment to see the producer or the director, and spend some time sorting out the problem. When I worked with Crawford's, poor old Hector was horrified at the end of the first year when I told him at a meeting that we'd changed much of all the scripts in *Matlock*. I did 192 scripts, and I went over every script. I never went out much to play golf or tennis on weekends, which I loved to do. I spent the weekend looking at the scripts I got sent to me ahead, and I would make notes and send them back to the producer or the director, and I would say, 'Please have a look at this scene'. And that's what I think a professional actor should do. You should use the benefit of whatever your experience is, relate that to the people you're working with, so that you improve the base product that you're all working on. If you don't do that, you shouldn't be in the business."

THE early 1960s saw television tighten its grip on Australian audiences. One by one, major metropolitan radio stations pulled drama off air. And one by one, Grace's competitors closed shop: Donovan Joyce, EMI, AWA, ART, Broadcast Exchange, and Fidelity. The Crawfords switched to television. Ironically, only Artransa — the company she founded for A. E. Bennett back in 1934 — still soldiered on, producing 52-episode self-contained half-hour programmes.

Wisely, Grace and Reg James switched the long-running shows onto "continuing" contracts, so that stations had to give three months' notice of cancellation in writing. When a show ended ahead of time, some stations just let the story stop unfinished, leaving their listeners high and dry. Other stations negotiated with James for a special closing episode to be written and recorded, so that the story could at least be resolved before it was taken off air.

Even in those grim times, Grace seized a new opportunity. She took over selling programmes for her competitors. Eventually she controlled most of the radio programmes that had ever been made in Australia, distributing the libraries of Donovan Joyce, AWA, EMI, Artransa, BEA, and ART around the world.

Donovan Joyce was the first competitor that Grace approached. "I don't think he knew why we wanted to take him over," admitted Reg James. "When I got excited about the prospects, I think he thought

I was stupid. A lot of his programmes had been sold to the Major network on a 5-year contract. Many were on 16-inch transcriptions, so we transferred them to tape. Because we had overseas markets, we did well out of them."

James also negotiated with AWA. "I remember when we took over AWA's programmes, I got their sales list. They hadn't sold a programme for three or four years, they hadn't been trying." James was shocked to discover that some of their top-rated shows like *The Air Adventures of Biggles* couldn't be sold again: too many episodes were missing, and too little care had been taken of those that survived.

Over a beer with Ken Johns of AWA and Bill Ramsey of EMI, Ramsey told James that he had a lot of shows available too. James went out with Ramsey to EMI at Homebush and sorted through the discs. "I didn't want the 2,276 episodes of *Dad and Dave*, because they were on 16-inch transcriptions. There were also whole batches of episodes missing. In one episode, Dave and Mabel were engaged and break up; in the next playable episode they had a baby. I guess they weren't as slow as we thought." (Ultimately it was 2UW's talkback star John Laws who revived *Dad and Dave* as memorabilia. 2UW bought the rights from EMI and edited 940 episodes down to 5-minuters for Laws's top-rating morning programme. Later, Gibson's bought the show from 2UW for $1 an episode, and sold it to many stations for $13 an episode in the 1980s. New Zealand paid $20 an episode.)

The EMI and ART libraries offered Grace the best resale opportunities. Because only a few copies of each episode survived, they had to be transferred to tape for distribution. It was worth the effort. Grace retained 50% of each sale.

Meanwhile, James grasped opportunities of his own like a true bowerbird. When 2UE moved out of Savoy House for new studios in North Sydney, he garnered all the old equipment he could lay hands on — even unwanted stocks of carbon paper.

AS THINGS got tougher, Grace needed an accountant with whom she could talk, someone who understood the business as well as she did. Baker Gilliver Robson had taken over from George Millar, but as the business contracted Grace found their fees too high.

Fred Mackay had been the accountant at 2UW's Fidelity Radio and had gone out on his own. He had good contacts with radio people. Reg James remembered him affectionately. "He was good for Grace and good for the company. He was always running, always in a hurry. He would drop in the pay and race for the door, but Grace was quicker. 'Fred...!' Fred would be summoned into Grace's office and emerge half an hour later."

Mackay once wanted to get rid of a lot of Grace's financial records that he had been holding. He brought them across to the despatch department in Savoy House and dropped them off behind the back door. Always in a hurry he dashed off, intending to phone James later and ask him to go down and collect them. Three days later he remembered and made the call. By that time, the caretaker had cleared all "the rubbish" and Grace's records were gone.

"Fred died in the loveliest way," said James. "He came back from lunch and keeled over. He had the happiest funeral."

After Mackay, Gordon Pole took over — a dour accountant who was so conservative that even Grace called him "*Mr* Pole".

THE downsizing of Grace Gibson Radio Productions was progressive.

Val Vine left in 1962 and was not replaced. Grace's long-time production manager Lawrence H. Cecil had also retired, and suffered a heart attack in 1963. John Saul took over as production manager and Eden Rutter directed shows, took over casting, as well as operated the panel. At that stage, the company was producing *Dr Paul, Portia Faces Life*, and a quarter-hour serial.

When Rutter left the business a few years later, Woodward combined her duties with his own. Eventually he was directing, operating the panel, cutting masters, maintaining equipment, casting, editing scripts, and doing all the cost sheets. He remembered how tough Grace was at audition stage. "She would read the scripts, I would read the scripts, there'd be a script conference, we'd go over it, and I'd be sent away to cast it. She would look at my choices, and approve the cast to go to audition stage. The audition episodes would be recorded and the whole office would sit in on judgement. The audition shows were so important because they were sent to the stations and that was what they bought the shows on."

AS RADIO stations dumped drama, they remained scrupulously ethical. When 2UE pulled *I Know My Love* off air, it honoured its contract to the letter and paid the full price for the 100 or so episodes it had never broadcast. It had also bought *Desiree*, a serial based on the life of Napoleon starring Amber Mae Cecil, scheduled to start in January 1963, by which time its Top 40 format was in full swing. It was paid for, but never broadcast.

However, 3AK Melbourne was a different story.

It had also bought *Desiree* for £5 an episode, and started playing it from 11 February 1963. When the station manager rang Grace and said he was cancelling the show, she told him he would have to pay for all 104 episodes.

"No, I won't," he said, "I haven't signed the contract."

Grace was livid. "You are joking."

For years, Grace had taken stations on trust. Discs were often sent out based on a verbal agreement; the formal written contract would follow later. It was the first time anyone had reneged. Eventually the station paid.

But the biggest blow was yet to come.

ON WEDNESDAY, 3 June 1964, Reg James made a hurried visit to 2UW Sydney, the station that continued broadcasting almost nothing but serials every weekday morning. He had heard a rumour that the station was about to abandon drama.

The manager Frank Jeffcoat was an old friend, but when James called into his office he was told that Jeffcoat was unavailable. Sensing that something was wrong, James put the question directly to his secretary Sheila Hogg. She denied the rumour emphatically. James returned to Hunter Street and told Grace, "They assured me they aren't taking the serials off."

The next morning 2UW played its serials as usual. Only when the last show had been broadcast was the announcement made. The inevitable had finally happened. All the dramas were being taken off air.

Minutes later Sheila Hogg was on the line. "I'm sorry, Reg, I was forbidden to tell you…"

James accepted her apology. "I wasn't upset with her. It was a terrible job for Frank. They didn't just have *Dr Paul* and *Portia Faces Life*. They had serials virtually wall-to-wall from 9 a.m. to 12 noon, Monday to Thursday. He had to take them all off…"

It was the end of an era.

IN ANOTHER part of the 2UW Building Alf Ward of Fidelity Radio, one of Grace's oldest competitors, invited James to call by and see him.

When James arrived, Ward led him into a storeroom full of his company's programmes. "Would you like to take them over?" Ward asked hopefully.

James looked round at the shelves piled high with ancient 16-inch pressings. Stations were not equipped to play them any more; their turntables were designed only for LPs. The cost and time of transferring thousands of hours of programmes from disc to tape would have been prohibitive, and James did not have enough space to store them. Besides which, only a handful of Fidelity's shows had any likely resale potential.

Sadly, James had to say no.

WHEN 2UW lifted the stylus on serials, *Dr Paul* had reached episode 3,101. The station was contracted to buy the show until episode 3,156 and had to pay for another 55 episodes, at £12 each, whether it broadcast them or not. The payment was made without fuss.

But Grace had a reprieve — a long reprieve, as it turned out. *Dr Paul* was still in production, still profitable, and still going to air across Australia on city and country stations. It was the Sydney market that needed her attention.

Her negotiations paid off.

Three months later, *Dr Paul* was back on air — this time on 2CH, oddly enough a station that had never been a heavy drama broadcaster. The story continued from episode 3,111 onwards, which was a suitable "opening" episode for the show's new broadcaster. 2CH paid £8 an episode, including the episodes that had already been paid for by 2UW. (The wheel had apparently turned full circle; two of Grace's earliest productions, *Here Are The Facts* and *Nyal Radio Playhouse*, had first aired on 2CH in the 1940s. Now, thirty years later, the station provided a lifeline for her flagship serial.)

In Melbourne, *Dr Paul* continued on 3DB. After the switch to decimal currency, the station was paying $22 an episode, "a good price" according to Reg James. (It wasn't until 1966 that 3DB cancelled the serial. The station's manager Curteis Crawford called Reg James with the news. *Dr Paul* was still attracting a large audience according to the survey, and under normal circumstances he would have kept the show on air. However, the station was changing its format, it was getting out of drama, and everything had to go. He was very sorry about it.)

1964 WAS Grace's year of living dangerously, and she wasted no time sending Reg James to New Zealand to sell ten new programmes to the New Zealand Broadcasting Corporation.

With the new contracts happily under his belt, James applied for holiday leave. Grace, however, had other plans.

She wanted him to go to South Africa, where television had yet to begin. The government's South African Broadcasting Corporation ran a commercial radio network, Springbok, which was a prime market for radio drama. Kenya, Rhodesia and Zambia were also key customers. The more sales she could secure, the easier it would be to offset losses in Australia. The timing was crucial.

As far as Grace was concerned, the matter was settled. "If you don't go to Africa, Reg, you can't have your holidays."

James patiently explained that he and his wife Neryl had everything planned. "I've got to have my holidays. We've booked in, we've paid our money, and we're going."

Grace fixed him with a look. "You've changed, Reg. Before you got married you never used to take holidays."

It was a stalemate. When he and Grace were mad at each other, James would go into his office and she would go into hers and they would not talk for a week. Finally she compromised. She would let James have his holiday if he agreed to go to South Africa at whatever time the South Africans specified as ideal. James agreed. "So help me, they nominated February, right when I was going on holidays. Perhaps she rung them up or wrote them a secret letter and suggested February. It was amazing how it worked out. I believed her. Now, in retrospect, I don't think I would."

So James packed his bags, said goodbye to a disappointed wife, and went to Africa on a lumbering DC6, stopping off in Adelaide and Perth on the way. In typical fashion, a victorious Grace never compensated him for his forfeited holiday payments.

Grace, however, did not always get her way. When his daughter was born, Grace wanted the baby named after her. Reg and Neryl James politely refused. Instead, they named her Glenys Grace. "Grace was quite happy with her initials, G.G."

ROSS Napier was another who found his life disrupted by Grace's whims. When his friends went off for tennis weekends, Grace kept him back writing. She used to take pleasure in asking, "Oh, you're going for a tennis weekend, are you, Ross?"

"Yes, Miss Gibson, I'm going to Wellington."

"You *were* going to Wellington," Grace corrected him.

But in 1964 the boot was on the other foot.

Napier was back in Australia, writing *Portia Faces Life* and two other shows for Grace. Grace, meanwhile, had headed off on a 3-month trip to London, America and the West Indies. She had no sooner gone than Napier was asked to write a new television series called *Skippy*.

It was what he had been waiting for — the chance to establish his name in the new medium. It was an offer he couldn't refuse. "I had to write her a very diplomatic letter and tell her what happened, and ask if she would excuse me, and did she suppose she could find someone else to take over. I couldn't have gone to Grace and said I'm not doing any more. No way I would have done that. I'd have jumped off the Bridge before I did that."

Napier had always addressed her as Miss Gibson. Penning her a letter for the first time he wrote, "Dear Grace..."

Fortunately, a Melbourne writer Tina Bethel was available to take over his assignments.

BY 1967, Grace Gibson Radio Productions had become a shadow of its former self — but a virile shadow nevertheless. Weathering the kind of cynicism she had first experienced when her company started, Grace developed new markets and new programmes.

One afternoon she climbed into a Rolls Royce, specially hired for the occasion. It journeyed across the Harbour Bridge to 2UE's new headquarters in North Sydney. She had an appointment to see the managing director Stewart Lamb and general manager Alan Faulkner. Under her arm were the audition episodes of a new comedy show from America called *Chickenman*. Grace had predicted it would be a smash hit with Australian audiences, and the two men eagerly awaited her arrival. For her part, Grace saw *Chickenman* as her way back into 2UE — and, if she had anything to do it, it was going to be a stylish return.

Chickenman was a serialised spoof of *Superman*, wherein a meek shoe salesman took on the guise of the feathered fighter who opposed crime on weekends. Each episode ran three-and-a-half minutes, around the length of the average pop song, and could easily slot into radio's new, faster formats. The show was the brainchild of Dick Orkin, whose Radio Ranch is still America's cutting edge radio commercial production house. Grace had imported 260 episodes of the comedy serial. All her instincts told her it couldn't fail.

Whatever Lamb and Faulkner had been expecting, they didn't hear it. They thought *Chickenman* was terribly unfunny. Grace was devastated. Comedy, it seemed, had failed her again. It had been the most humiliating afternoon of her life. For the first time in her career, her magic had failed her, and never again would she attempt to sell another programme in person.

It took time, but eventually Grace's instincts were vindicated.

5AD Adelaide picked up the show, then 3DB Melbourne. One by one other capital city markets followed, and soon *Chickenman* was Australia's hottest new radio show everywhere but Sydney. Grudgingly 2UE admitted it might have been wrong. A year after Grace's fruitless trip in the Rolls, *Chickenman* went to air on that station in November 1968, but in the worst possible time slot — 8.30 p.m. The programme virtually died.

And it would have vanished without trace, were it not for the innovative young programme director at 2UW, Ray Bean. Bean had started as a programmer at 2KY in 1956, the year TV arrived and the Top 40 format revolutionised radio. "So many stations wouldn't recognise that radio, in the form it had been in for some years, would change. When I went to 2UW, it was almost wall-to-wall serials. There was a lot of stubbornness at 2UW. You had people who had been there for years and years and years. They said, oh, music will never succeed, people want more than music, and they were well and truly proved wrong." Thanks to the transistor, radio pursued a younger, more mobile audience. And Bean, like Grace, grasped *Chickenman's* potential.

Immediately *Chickenman* finished on 2UE, Bean rang Reg James and bought the show for $7 an episode. They cut a deal allowing Bean to broadcast each episode twice a day, once in morning drive time and again in the evening, starting 30 October 1972. It was the smash hit that Grace had predicted. According to Bean, "It was a fairly crazy show and our audience seemed to respond to that. 2UE, even though it was a Top 40 station, was a very conservative station in many respects, so they really didn't want to take a chance. We took it up and it fitted in to the crazy format we were going into, and away it went."

As ever, Grace knew when she was on a good thing, and quickly imported more American short shows — 2,600 episodes of psychologist Dr Joyce Brothers talking about sex for three and a half minutes, Earl Nightingale's motivational talk series *Our Changing World*, and *The Passing Parade*, true stories narrated by the sonorous John Doremus. Of the latter, Grace had imported the first 130 shows. When she went back for more, Doremus confessed the show had failed in the States. So Ross Napier was called in, and for the first time in radio history, 1,350 Australian scripts were sent to America for recording.

GRACE continued to walk a tightrope through 1968. Quarter-hour shows were still selling, and new, shorter shows were being developed. But the old glory days were long gone, and one event in particular brought that fact home.

When Lawrence H. Cecil died at 79, only Grace and her staff went to the funeral. Nobody attended from Macquarie or 2GB. His ten years at the helm of the network's great dramas were all but forgotten. His death was especially sad for Val Vine. "He said to me once, 'You must meet my daughter.' I met her all right. We were the two youngies on the block." Vine and actress Amber Mae Cecil became close friends. "She was Matron of Honour at both my marriages, and Grace asked me, 'Do you have Amber Mae at all your weddings?'"

INCREDIBLY, Grace's two flagship quarter-hour serials continued in production for another two years.

Dr Paul finally took down his shingle in July 1970. "Not because of lack of sales," Reg James pointed out, "but because we could not find good scripts or writers. Indeed we'd started on another storyline, and produced up to episode 4,644 when the decision was made to stop. I went back and found an episode where the story could possibly finish, and finish quickly." As a result, eight recorded episodes never went to air.

With stations cancelling *Portia Faces Life* almost weekly, it was decided to feature the character Portia Manning in shorter-running serials, which she would also narrate. They were *Portia* stories, but provided stations the flexibility to play them as separate serials with their own titles. The test case was 128 quarter-hour episodes called *The Haverlock Affair*. New Zealand bought it, profits were assured, and *Portia* could continue. Then came 104 episodes of *Partners in Jeopardy* and *Thirty Days Hath September*, 128 episodes of *The Silent Witness*, two 130-episode shows *Violets Are Blue* and *Clayton Place*. *The Seed of Evil* ran for 52 episodes.

Sales were also maintained through the old catalogue and the programmes of Grace's former competitors. As well, new programmes were sourced from overseas producers of comedy, talk, music and drama. Mostly these organisations were US-based, although shows came from England, Scotland, South Africa, Canada and New Zealand. James remembered being offered a serial produced in the West Indies, "but the accents would not have been understood in Australia".

IN 1971 Grace moved out of City Mutual. 2UE, 2SM and dozens of advertising agencies had already abandoned the expensive central business district and relocated to the northside. It was also time to sever the old links with Savoy House where the despatch department was still located. It was a reluctant decision; Grace had spent all her business life in a two-block radius of Bligh and Hunter Streets. Her social life was also centred in the area: the American Club, the Pickwick Club, and her much-loved Elizabeth Street restaurant, The Normandie. As a friend remarked, she had probably never ventured farther south than Market Street!

She chose offices and built a studio at ADC House on the Pacific Highway at North Sydney, directly opposite the railway station. The staff was ecstatic. In Savoy House and City Mutual, they had had no windows. Now, from both sides, they had harbour views; one looked across the Bridge to the city, the other out to the Heads.

Typically, John Woodward and Reg James were pressed into service as removalists. Together they shifted carloads of files, transcription discs and equipment. The big moving day was a Saturday when the entire control room from Hunter Street was transplanted in North Sydney. They worked all morning, and Grace and Ronnie arrived with sandwiches and liquor. Everyone who wanted a beer was allowed one. "For some reason I was given two," recalled Reg James, "possibly because John didn't drink."

Grace Gibson Radio Productions was now just Grace, Woodward, James, Noreen Tweeddale, and a receptionist. And, of course, the tea lady. A war widow, Mrs Cox also unwrapped the parcels and put all the discs away. But there were no typists and no stencils — the writers' scripts were simply photocopied for the casts.

A small office next to reception and the switchboard had been reserved for Ronnie. As Grace had recently had a new portrait of herself painted by June Mendoza, the original by Judy Cassab now hung on its wall. It measured four feet by two, and overpowered the small space. As much as Ronnie loved Grace, it would have been too much to have to look at it for hours on end. While he happily drove her to and from North Sydney each day, he rarely came upstairs to his office. (When Grace sold the company, she presented the portrait to James. And as much as he admired Grace, the painting proved equally impossible to hang in his home!)

Nor did James settle into his new office easily. Because his despatch department provided such a stunning view of Middle Harbour, Grace maintained he couldn't have views on both sides of the building; she allocated him a small office at the end of a corridor. Relations were strained for a week or so, but he did end up with the best of both worlds — she allowed him to use her office when entertaining clients and whenever she wasn't there. It was typical of Grace; although she bawled him out for smoking, drinking, using too much Scotch at parties and spending too much on new transcriptions, their disagreements rarely lasted.

North Sydney offered other compensations for the staff beyond the views. Grace had discovered a restaurant called Christopher's in the next building. It soon became a firm favourite and usually she took the staff with her for lunch, particularly if they convinced her they were hungry.

It was now that Grace took her first and only trip on a train. She journeyed from North Sydney to Wynyard to visit 2GB's new home in Sussex Street, where she renewed friendships with staff she had worked with forty years ago.

GRACE's new premises ushered in a new era.

She devised a new radio concept: the mini-drama, a serial broadcast weekly in five four-minute episodes. As the publicity blurb promised:

Here is the new concept in programming for stations, irrespective of their style or format.

These four-minute serials provide drama in the modern manner ... believable characters ... a climax in every episode ... with story lines taken from all walks of life.

Initially, Grace had intended utilising old scripts from *Night Beat* and her courtroom dramas, adapting and editing them for the new, shorter shows, but Ross Napier disagreed. He maintained that only original stories, specially conceived to work in the new format, would do the job. He won the argument.

ON 11 October 1971, the first Grace Gibson mini-drama went to air in the Sydney market. At $14 an episode, 2UE was playing *I Killed Grace Random*.

"And it succeeded," said Reg James, "because 2UE broadcast it on the top-rating Bob Rogers show. It proved so successful that in 1985, 2WS played a repeat performance."

Grace was excited. Radio drama was back in a big way, defying all the experts. "We took these sort of things for granted," said James. "We had an absolute belief in radio drama. It was just coming up with the idea."

I Killed Grace Random was the story of a hit-and-run accident, adapted by Ross Napier from Elleston Trevor's novel, starring Richard Meikle and June Salter. Kurt, played by Richard Meikle, is an advertising executive driving home late at night. Suddenly a figure flashes in front of his car. He runs her down but doesn't stop. As the story unfolds he becomes more and more obsessed with the dead girl's face. Eventually he comes up with a road safety campaign using the girl's photo. In the end, not even the police believe his confession.

The show was playing smoothly when suddenly 2UE baulked at a line of dialogue.

It came in a scene at the advertising agency. A colleague said to Kurt, "You're obsessed with this girl. You must be sleeping with her." And Kurt snapped back, "You bastard, you're a bastard."

2UE refused to play it.

"They didn't like the word 'bastard' and they didn't like 'sleeping with her'," recalled James. "So we had to cut those two lines of dialogue for 2UE and give them their episode on tape. But it was so mild — it was two men, in a private office, talking as men do, and Kurt's reaction was that of an obsessed man. But we *had* to change it."

The four-minute serials with continuing stories each ran for 130 suspense-packed episodes in which every word counted. *I Killed Grace Random*, *My Father's House*, and *Without Shame* defied all predictions, playing in every capital city as well as a vast country network. Grace's concept had been simple enough. Three minutes was too short for a drama, but in four minutes enough of the story could be developed. And she was right.

The 1973 mini-drama, We, *The Wicked People*, broke more new ground. It offered a complete story weekly in five four-minute episodes. It also ran for 260 episodes, enough for a year's airplay. As the publicity promised:

> Lucas, a columnist with the Evening Standard, tells tense, exciting stories that prove there is a little wickedness in us all.

Before the Court was another mini-drama with stories self-contained within five four-minute episodes.

RADIO serials had not only sped up, they had also been spiced up. The new mini-dramas were a far cry from the old shows about clergymen and doctors.

In 1973, Ross Napier wrote *Without Shame*, the story of Judith Farrow, a woman whose husband makes love to her sister, the husband

and sister are murdered, she gets the blame, and is sent to prison. "All that happens in the first five episodes," observed Reg James. However, once Judith Farrow is incarcerated in gaol, Napier's intention was to introduce a lesbian warder to the story. When Reg James consulted 2GB manager Percy Campbell about the idea, Campbell turned white and said no.

As James recalled, "At about that time a reporter interviewed me about radio drama, so I played them the first episodes of *Without Shame*, and out comes the *Sun-Herald* with a front page headline 'Radio Goes Naked'."

Another of Napier's scripts, *Portia Faces Life*, disturbed Hamilton Huntley, the general manager of 2CH whose call sign was an acronym for Church. James remembered the incident. "Writers always had the licence to put what they wanted into a script, and it was our job to say whether it was acceptable or not. The language they used gave the impression of what the character was like, how they would speak in a given situation. Ross wrote a scene in a court case, where the woman was being badgered by the defence attorney and called every kind of slut, and she just emoted 'You bastard, you rotten bastard'."

As the episode was to be broadcast on 2CH, the decision was made to show the script to Huntley, and see what he had to say. Huntley's answer was a compromise: "Well, let's just do *one* 'bastard'."

When Grace was given the news back at the office, she retorted: "If you're going to do one bastard, you might as well do two!"

So, two "bastards" it was.

Nobody told Huntley. As the weeks ticked by and the airdate grew closer, James calculated to his horror that the episode would be played on Easter Monday. *Two "bastards", on a church station, on Easter Monday!* James made sure he was listening, but the suspense was too much. He had to find out how many complaints the station had received before Huntley rang him to complain.

James enlisted his wife's help. Neryl James rang the station, not to complain, but to ask if she had really heard them broadcast the word "bastard". The announcer spoke to Neryl for a good ten minutes, and she was the only one who had called. "Which meant," surmised James, "either no one was offended, or no one was listening."

BY THE mid-1970s Grace could proudly declare that at least sixty per cent of her revenue then came from overseas sales. In fact, in most English-speaking broadcasting markets, Grace Gibson was the BBC Transcription Service's sole competitor.

"Grace was a survivor of the most inspiring kind," said Alan White. "Always upbeat, always enthusiastic, and always demanding of the highest standards — a perfectionist."

She was also an inveterate bean counter. From time to time she would call in Reg James and ask, "Tell me, how much have we got back on *Dossier on Dumetrius*?"

Oddly enough, Grace was always paranoid that her old stars would discover that the shows for which they had been paid £1 an episode were still being sold around the world, and still raking in profits. There had been no such things as residuals in the old days, and Grace owned all the rights. Yet she could have set her mind at rest. Everybody knew.

Dinah Shearing called by at the office in the late 1970s and heard John Woodward dubbing an episode of *Dossier on Dumetrius*. She poked her head into the control room. "John, don't tell me you're still selling *that*..."

Shearing had received countless letters over the years from friends "in all sorts of places like Canada and the Channel Islands" saying they had heard her voice. In fact, on a voyage through the Panama Canal, Shearing had gone ashore with her youngest son Matthew and caught a cab. "When the cab came to a stop, Matt suddenly said, 'There you are, Mummy,' and I said, 'What, darling?' And he said, 'That's you'. And I said, 'What's me?' And suddenly I could hear a bit of *Dr Paul* playing, drifting in from a radio in a shop. Grace must have made a fortune out of all of us…"

Peter Yeldham recalled a phone call from a British writer on *The Troubleshooters*. "He'd just got back from Tahiti in the early 1970s. Apparently he'd been lying on the beach listening to the radio when on came a radio drama with my name in the opening credits. He said, 'I'm ringing you so you can get on to them and get your royalties.' And I said, 'Listen, I've got news for you…'"

Over lunch one day, actor Ray Barrett said to Grace, "If I had even half a dollar for every show I was in that you sold overseas, I'd be rich now."

"You're right," said Grace, "you would be."

EVEN in the mid-1970s Grace could still profitably produce new quarter-hour serials. *Under Her Spell* ran 130 episodes, playing five days a week for 26 weeks across Australia. James Condon, Fay Kelton and Diana Perryman were the stars. The economics were interesting.

It went to air in 1973. The first sale was to 2RE Taree for $1 an episode. Darwin paid $1.80. Hobart was the only capital city to run the serial, paying $4. A national sale to New Zealand returned $30 an episode and guaranteed profits. Other foreign sales soon followed: Trinidad paid $4.25, and Radio Jacaranda in Rhodesia, $3.75. In 1974, Singapore was paying $5 an episode. The show played in Guyana, Radio Dominica, Cook Islands, Fiji, Bermuda, Belize, Cayman, and Norfolk Island, and the last sale was to New Guinea — in 1986.

"For some reason, in the office we used to call it 'Under Her Whatsit'," recalled Reg James. "The scriptwriter, James Aitchison writing under the pseudonym David Carrick, was paid $12 an episode and the actors $4 each." But the lower fees meant actors had to be accommodated. When the star James Condon took on a play at The Independent theatre, he was scheduled to miss three weeks of recording. So in the serial he was knocked down by a car and over the next 15 episodes all listeners heard were his pre-recorded groans from a hospital bed.

A series of 90-second "capsules" narrated by Alastair Duncan generated additional revenue. Duncan revisited famous crimes in *A Murder A Minute*, and gave clues to famous landmarks in *Discover the World*.

Dr Paul was still playing in 1973, but stations were paying less and less. 2XL Cooma paid 95 cents an episode. 2AD Armidale, 2LF Young, and 2MO Gunnedah paid $1, and 7QT Queensland, $1.25. "We were happy to break even," said James, "and no one could deny radio drama was still there."

Until it sank, *Dr Paul* was even playing on a British pirate radio station.

In the West Indies meantime, *Dr Paul* and Grace Gibson were the most widely recognised Australian icons — the only exception being Australia's test cricketers.

TWENTY years after the arrival of television, Grace recorded her last quarter-hour serial — *A Relative Affair*.

It went to air in October 1977 over 7HO Hobart, 7EX Launceston, 4BU Bundaberg, 4ZR Roma, and 2CA Canberra. As usual, sales to Radio Jamaica, Radio Trinidad, Bermuda, the Bahamas, Montserrat, Barbados, Antigua, Cayman Islands, Fiji and Singapore covered production costs and ensured a good profit.

By then, Reg James recalled, "the actors' fees had got too high for radio, and they just didn't have the time."

But a lot of them still hankered to do more serials. Calling in to the office, June Salter told Grace, "Oh, if you want to make another serial, count me in. I'd love to do it."

Wendy Playfair was another. "I wish you'd do some more serials. I loved working in them."

WHEN the Yeldhams returned to Sydney in 1976 they had lunch with Grace. They saw her several times at the penthouse after that — there'd be a companionable round of drinks, before going over the road for a meal.

"Once I'd got over my fear and awe of her, I liked her very much." Yeldham described her as warm, tough, and likeable. "We were what she called 'the talent', the writers and actors, and I thought she was pretty good with all of us really." Yeldham believed she did a lot for the industry as well as for him personally. "Others did, too, but in the end I think I preferred working for Grace than most of the others. She used to like to talk about what you wrote. She's ring up and say, 'I don't like that guy on page 23.' And I'd say, 'You weren't meant to like him, Grace.' And she'd say, 'Oh, I see…' "

Grace kept in touch with Val Vine, too. "I think I got to know her better away from the office," Vine reflected. "We used to chat a lot. She used to ring me some nights at about half past nine or quarter to ten. She used to watch the serials on TV, and she loved *Peyton Place*. I miss her terribly, a great deal. I think anyone who knew Grace, and was close to her, would miss her."

RADIO drama had reached its peak during Australia's age of innocence. Its impact on Australian life had been immeasurable.

"Television is so all-consuming in its way," reflected Ross Napier. "Television shows it all. Once you've seen a TV show, you've seen it. You forget it. Radio doesn't show it. You just hear those voices, and you put all sorts of wild imaginings to them. It's a tremendous attraction because they're a mystery, and they remain a mystery. I've always maintained this is what makes radio such a tremendous medium. It's still got the pull as much as it ever did. Even more so."

Grace had extended radio drama's shelf life by a good twenty years. Incredibly, one of the best shows was yet to come.

Episode 12

And so ends our story

IT WAS 1978. Grace Gibson Radio Productions was in its thirty-fourth year. Grace had produced 200 different shows; 37 had used American scripts, the rest had been written by Australians.

Grace and Ronnie made their final visit to the States where she spent a number of weeks in hospital recovering from an overdose of drugs.

"She had become a drug addict in the sense that she went to so many different doctors, they all gave her tablets to take, but she did not tell them that she had received medication from other doctors," Reg James recalled. "She was taking this great mixture into her system. She said she had a bad heart, but her doctor here, a top man, said she didn't. On one occasion she went to a doctor in Honolulu and he said, 'Your Sydney doctor is right, you do not have a bad heart.'"

When Grace returned to Sydney, James believed she was ready to give it all away.

"She was just tired and worn out. She'd had a number of operations for cancer, always when she was in the United States. We didn't ever believe she had cancer, and I must admit we doubted the necessity for another operation. She was weak, she was old, she was 73, she'd had a tough life."

But not too weak to call Ross Napier and brief him on his most difficult assignment. "I had to write their obituaries, Grace's and Ronnie's.

It was the worst job I had to do, well before they died. She wanted it all ready. She sent me all this stuff I never knew about. It was all sort of contradictory. I could never figure it all out."

Grace was winding down, and so was the company. Hundreds of her old transcriptions had been despatched to the National Film and Sound Archive of Australia in Canberra. But many were still playing, somewhere in the world.

Giving up, though, was not in Grace's character. First, she had to find a way out.

KEITH Graham was about to open 2WS, the first new AM radio licence granted in Sydney in 46 years. Graham and one of his directors talked to Reg James about buying Grace's company. But their workload was too great at that stage, they couldn't take anything else on, and the talks were aborted.

In the meantime an American radio producer approached Grace with an offer to buy the company.

"It was a terrible time for her," James recounted. "She didn't know what to do. She was concerned about the staff, about Noreen, and John, and me."

Grace's brother Calvin was visiting Sydney with his wife at the time and they were keen for her to sell. They talked to James and asked if he would be prepared to stay with the company after it was sold. "I was the only person who knew all the programmes, and the selling and marketing of them. They said nobody would buy the company without me going along with it." James promised Grace he would stay on and help the new owner. Company secretary Gordon Pole prepared the documents. Everything was set.

Then from America came demands for all sorts of guarantees.

"He thought he could put pressure on Grace and get the company without paying a dollar," James concluded. "In the end I cabled him and said, send the money or the deal's off. No money arrived so the deal was off."

When the sale fell through, Grace was keen for her three old staffers to buy the business on very good terms. But it wasn't to be.

The uncertainty persisted through most of 1978, until suddenly the end was in sight.

In early August, James took a call from Canberra. Nick Erby, the general manager of 2CC, was on the line. 2CC was the newly licenced second commercial radio station in Canberra, owned by Capital City Broadcasters.

"Nick was a radio drama believer, and had been 2UE's programme director when the mini-dramas first went to air. He knew our product from 2UE, and from Moree and Toowoomba. He had a love of radio drama and was a young rebel in broadcasting — he went to industry meetings without a coat and tie. He asked whether I thought Grace would sell to his company. I kept him on the phone and raced into Grace and asked her, 'Would you sell?' She said, 'Yes, I'd like to,' so I ran back and told Nick, 'Yes, she'll talk.'"

Two days later, James was in Canberra. Erby introduced him to the board. They agreed to buy the business on the spot, subject to price.

James knew they were close to a sale. The directors came up to meet with Grace and settled the deal a couple of weeks later. "Grace was happy, she was very comfortable with selling to Australians who shared her passion for radio drama."

By the end of August, Grace had retired. Ronnie was delighted. At last they could spend more time together.

"She was always there on the phone, ready to give advice, even if I didn't want it, though most of the time I did," said James. He asked Grace for her desk. Today his son, who was close to Grace, still uses it. "He used to put the scripts together in his school holidays at North Sydney."

Retirement brought some unexpected adjustments for Grace.

She was shocked when Sir Edwin Hicks, the chairman of Capital City Broadcasters, gave her back her car; it had never occurred to her that her Mercedes-Benz, one of her company's assets, was part of the sale.

The cost of living was another surprise. "The company had covered all her living expenses for years, even her phone bills and her petrol," said James. "So she had to come to terms with that…"

THE ink was no sooner dry than Nick Erby and Reg James headed to the States in search of new product.

James found the younger man's passion invigorating. "Nick had big ideas. He immediately sat down and wrote a serial called *The Priestman File*, about a man who wanted to be Prime Minister of Australia. Nick wrote 30 six-minute episodes, but we made him write 65. He directed the show. It set a pattern, gave us a start." The show went to air in February 1981.

James also found himself able to penetrate the inner sanctum of the broadcasting industry. Now that a broadcasting station owned Grace Gibson Radio Productions, James could attend the annual closed-door convention of the Federation of Australian Radio Broadcasters. It were as though the wheel had come full circle; FARB was the latter day version of the old Federation which Grace's mentor, A. E. Bennett, had founded back in 1930.

Instead of having to drive from one country station to another, James had a suite in which he entertained delegates and played them shows. One manager drank so much he came back the next morning and asked James what shows he had ordered. Another got back to his room so late that his wife refused to let him in.

IT WAS time for one last hurrah. *Castlereagh Line* was one of the most popular Grace Gibson shows of all. It ran for 910 six-minute episodes and was broadcast in every radio market in Australia and most of the company's overseas markets. "We even looked like selling it in the US," admitted James, "but it was decided the Aussie language went a little too far for American listeners to comprehend."

Erby had read Don Whitington's book *King Hit*. Erby gave it to James and he passed it to Ross Napier who also saw its potential. "By the time we started production in 1982," recalled James, "Nick had left the company and gone to Melbourne. But we carried on, virtually the old Grace Gibson team, Ross Napier, John Woodward and I, without Grace, but in the Grace Gibson tradition. Grace watched our progress very closely."

Napier bought the radio rights himself. He not only wrote the serial, but also fulfilled a lifelong ambition by directing it.

First he spent a week or two looking over the locations where the story was set — in the old coaching stations around Tamworth and Glen Innes. Then he wrote a theme song to the tune of *Lilly Bolero* (also known as *Lillibullero*, an Irish melody used by the BBC World Service as its signature theme). The song would open each episode together with the sound of a Cobb & Co coach. John Woodward recalled, "The only available sound effects were a horse-drawn sulky, things like that, while the Cobb & Coach coaches were pulled by a string of horses. I scoured Sydney looking for the sound. Eventually I went back to our own resources and I multiple-dubbed the horses until I had the right sound."

Napier also wanted the show produced in the style of a film production, recording scenes out of sequence. And to achieve a more contemporary stereo sound, something more akin to a Dolby movie soundtrack, the show was recorded at Gibson's but digitally mixed at the Madrigal studio in North Sydney. "I would take a pile of tapes to Madrigal," said Woodward, "all numbered, this scene is for episode 2, this scene is for episode 10."

It was the first time a major Gibson show had been digitally produced. "We were aspiring for excellence," said Napier. But the learning curve was steep. Napier was horrified to hear sound effects occasionally change perspective on air. "A cow supposedly mooing in a field sounded more like it was in bed with the heroine." Hisses and sibilance dogged the dialogue. Worse, the effects seemed to change from station to station. Instead of stereo sound, sometimes the show only came through one speaker.

Despite the glitches, Napier achieved his goals. Not only did audiences overwhelmingly respond to the show, the actors did too.

"The actors did not look down on radio, they wanted to do it," said James. "When we were casting *Castlereagh Line*, we were told that we'd never get the people for the money we were going to pay. But we worked out ways, because they all wanted to come in and do it. It was good training for them, too. People like Belinda Giblin became very big in *Castlereagh Line*, when she was already very big in television. She loved it. Her acting improved so much once she started doing radio and working with people like Ric Hutton, who was a past master of the art of radio acting. I remember one scene where Ric had a pencil in his mouth when he was talking, because he was meant to be eating, and all these young actors were looking at him unbelievably. Fancy putting a pencil in your mouth…" According to James, there was another lesson for the younger actors. "Ric hated his role in *Castlereagh Line*. He played a drunk, a rapist, and Ric was a very gentle person who really couldn't accept playing this role. But it was his job and he did it. He was excellent."

At a time when radio drama had long been unfashionable, it took a brave programmer to start the ball rolling in Sydney.

Enter Ray Bean, programme director of 2WS. Bean, who had seen the potential of *Chickenman* at 2UW, bought *Castlereagh Line* for the new Western Sydney station. As he explained, "The philosophy of the station then was very much to support Australian content. Our programming objective was to play contemporary Australian music, at a time when Australian music was still having a battle getting content to air." The same philosophy embraced drama. The station wanted local drama in its lineup; the problem was finding the correct product. "We could see that the right material would work very well. In the old days of drama it was the 15-minute session, but of course radio had moved to a tighter format. The old serials faded out because people didn't have time to sit down and listen to them. *Dr Paul* and *Portia Faces Life* and all those things were very old in their style and content, they'd had their day." Instead, Bean was keen to experiment with short dramas. His judgement proved correct.

Ironically, Bean had been programme director at 2UW when serials were dropped and had the task of introducing a new format. He succeeded then, and now when the wheel turned, he succeeded again.

BY THE time 2WS committed to *Castlereagh Line*, the serial was already playing on 61 stations around Australia and overseas.

Reg James believed one of the key selling points had been the company's guarantee of a logical conclusion every 65 episodes. Very few stations stopped before episode 910, and most wanted the story to continue, but writer-director Ross Napier called a halt.

At one metropolitan station, programme staff had considered a six-minute episode too long; they believed listeners would "tune out". Instead, they argued for a commercial break in the middle, but James stuck to his guns. Six minutes or no sale!

MONEY was never important if someone loved radio. Reg James wanted to do a two-hour Xmas show with Ita Buttrose. The budget for her was only $300, and she was keen. But her agent Harry M. Miller said no way, it had to be $600. The show was scrapped.

Three weeks later, Buttrose was on the phone to James.

"What's happened about the Christmas show, Reg?"

"Well, Harry said you can't do it," James told her. "We're not paying enough."

Buttrose didn't care. "I'll tell Harry I'll do it. When do you want me?"

GRACE had had an operation. One Saturday morning at 6 a.m., James received a phone call from the matron at St Luke's Private Hospital.

"Miss Gibson can't sleep," the matron told him, "and she would like you to go to her penthouse and bring her mattress to the hospital."

James was stunned. "Do you allow that?"

"No," confessed the matron, "but on this occasion we will permit it."

Fortunately James had a station wagon. He and his small son drove to the Macleay Regis, saw the caretaker, and bundled Grace's mattress downstairs. At St Luke's, he took off the hospital mattress and replaced it with hers.

Grace was delighted. She offered him a drink, and produced a bottle of Johnnie Walker. Then she opened a cupboard and poured herself a glass of Old Parr.

"I didn't mind drinking Johnnie Walker," conceded James. "I knew I wouldn't get the Old Parr, and Grace wasn't embarrassed in any way about me knowing what she was doing."

Grace survived her operation, but too many old friends were dying. Her producer, John Saul, signed off in 1979.

Two years later Ronnie followed.

"SHE was finished the day he died," said James. "She really didn't want to go on."

Ronnie's decline had been rapid. He had retained his faculties reasonably well, but an athletic lifetime had left him exhausted. He was placed in St Luke's Private Hospital where Grace visited every day; James was also a regular visitor, after which he had to report to Grace on Ronnie's condition. James and his wife Neryl often picked up Grace and Ronnie and drove them to Centennial Park for a chat in the open air.

Grace herself told an interviewer at the time: "I had the most wonderful husband, you couldn't find a more devoted husband. I've had a lot of sickness unfortunately in the last six or seven years, and he'd been by my side the whole time. I wouldn't be here if it weren't for him."

James asked her for something of Ronnie's as a keepsake and she gave him his watch. "Then, every time she used to see me, she'd put her hand on my wrist and hold on to the watch."

Ronnie's funeral service was held at St Stephens in Macquarie Street. The staff and society friends attended. Val Vine accompanied Grace. "It was her grief. She loved this man and she wanted the very best for him. She adored Ronnie, he was the light of her life and when he died, the light went out for her. We all miss him. He was like a dad — a gentle soul, a very good-looking man. As wild as she was, and she was a human dynamo, whenever she looked at Ronnie you could see the love in her eyes. It was lovely for us, as girls growing up, because we all wanted someone who looked like Ronnie."

Grace asked James and Napier if they would go to the Northern Suburbs crematorium with Ronnie. Noreen Tweeddale took Grace back to the penthouse.

GRACE loved her penthouse. It had been her home for a quarter of a century. There, a party for 100 people had been nothing. It was an "absolute dream", said a friend. Grace could relax in her large chair surrounded by a well-cared-for rooftop garden overlooking magnificent views of Sydney Harbour. It was a safe, serene environment, an opulent Shangri-La suspended over a vice pit.

Val Vine described the penthouse as Grace's gaol. "Grace became the victim of her beautiful home. It was in the heart of downtown Kings

Cross. She thought it was unsafe to go out, and she was right. She said to me one night, 'There's no point having the beautiful jewellery I've got. You can't wear it when you get older. I'm frightened I'd be mugged.' She was trapped in that house."

One night Grace was attending the Black and White Ball. It had been well documented that she was going to be a judge at the event. Grace threw a beautiful new white fox coat across the bed before she left. A cat burglar, watching from the roof, took the fur and many other valuables. Before Ronnie died, there had been a murder in the Macleay Regis, which shook both of them.

Once a week, Noreen Tweeddale called by to do the accounts. Tweeddale had never been happy at the company after Grace left. She became Grace's companion, chatting about golf and the old days. She typed letters to family members, did the day-to-day banking, and they always finished up with a gin and tonic or two.

Grace called Michael Pate and he went to see her. "She wanted me to have some of Ronnie's shoes, which she thought I'd look good in. I dropped in and we had a cup of coffee. Ronnie had been an immaculate dresser and he had some wonderful slip-ons. I took a couple of things just to please her and I think that was the last time I ever saw her."

IN HER final years, Grace was great company. Reg James took a journalist over to interview her. They arrived at eleven in the morning. The penthouse was bathed with sunlight and the harbour was dotted with white sails. Grace offered them wine. "It was actually a very lovely day. It was quite special to listen to Grace when she got talking."

Grace could look back on a very full life:

"I'm very happy with the life that's gone before me. I did as much as I could in the time. We certainly became the leading producer of dramatic radio shows in Australia, and the world as far as that goes. There's no company that I've ever heard of that produced 66 quarter-hours a week, so I'm very happy about the past. I've had a very good life and I'm proud of the organisation that I built up and proud of the shows that we produced. I think if you put our dramatic shows up against the dramatic shows that are on television today they would show up a lot better, because the scripts were good in those days."

Grace believed that the broadcasting authorities should have set a small quota for stations to play Australian-produced radio drama. She felt that a lot of people who used to listen to radio had given it away. She and Ronnie had enjoyed listening to some of the talkback shows, but as far as the standard of radio today was concerned, she was adamant. "It's so different that you couldn't call it radio. The programmes today aren't radio as we knew it at all. And if you look at the programme listings in the paper, which I often do, I think, oh my God…" Asked if she would work in radio now, she crisply observed, "No, I wouldn't care for that at all. I'm not a rock'n'roll fan or anything like that."

WITH 2WS committed to *Castlereagh Line*, Reg James believed the station was ready to buy the company. James favoured it. Erby, his ally at Capital City Broadcasters, had left. His replacement had proved uninspiring. On the other hand, Keith Graham and Ray Bean at 2WS were stalwart supporters and offered the leadership the company needed.

So, in late 1983, when the chairman of Capital City Broadcasters rang him and said, "Reg, I've got something to tell you, you'd better sit down, we've sold the company," James thought to himself, *"You beauty, Keith's bought us!"*

But the chairman's next words were a complete shock: "You're now owned by the Albert family of 2UW." And James did sit down.

When he called 2WS with the news, Keith Graham was stunned. "I knew somebody else was after it, but not them."

The Alberts had known Grace for years, and Sir Alexis Albert had been a personal friend all her life. The family controlled 2UW, a music recording studio, and a music publishing company. Grace believed it would be a very harmonious relationship, but by the early 90s the owners would start divesting themselves of their media interests.

Christmas 1983 brought news of a different kind. Betty Barnard, who had played such a significant role in Grace's life and been a valuable part of the company, had died.

FORTY years after Grace first hung out her shingle, production continued.

After *Castlereagh Line* came another six-minute serial, *Time Is The Catcher*, produced in 1984. It ran for 130 episodes and was written by veteran Russ Writer. Sales were good and included Radio Manx on the Isle of Man, some rural stations in New Zealand, and Montserrat in the West Indies.

While the success of *Castlereagh Line* paved the way for more six-minute serials, Reg James could not find suitable scriptwriters to keep up the supply. "The solution was to take our four-minute serials produced in the 1970s and join two episodes together. By deleting the opening and closing tracks, we achieved a six-minute duration. Instead of running 130 episodes, the new versions would run 65 episodes. It meant a little less revenue, but prices increased to compensate."

Once those serials had been "recycled", the bold step was taken to edit such timeless classics as *Cattleman* and the Gregory Keen serials to the new six-minute format. Each of the original episodes had a playing time of 12 minutes; by deleting the opening and closing tracks and dividing the episode into two parts, the old shows worked in the new six-minute format. "Again we were successful," reported James. "*Cattleman* ran for 416 six-minute episodes, double its original duration, while Gregory Keen's adventures each ran for 208. Listeners accepted them."

And, with a final twist of irony, the company revisited *Castlereagh Line* and joined two six-minute episodes together — thus converting it to a quarter-hour serial!

WITH the Alberts at the helm, there was a move afoot to turn their Brisbane station into a drama station. Much to everyone's surprise, James opposed the idea. "The station's general manager asked me to prepare a paper on the programmes that were available, which I did, but he was most surprised that I was against the idea. He was obviously against it, but thought I'd be so much in favour of it because radio drama was my business. But my business was ensuring that when radio drama went on air, it was accepted and enjoyed, and got *further* sales. I didn't believe that an audience, without ever having been exposed to radio drama, would listen to old shows. 1950s drama in 1980 wouldn't work. People had lost the art of listening. A TV car chase lasts half the episode and there's no dialogue. But in radio we relied on painting the picture through dialogue, through character. The writer had to write character, so that the character could develop."

On Christmas Eve 1984, the company vacated North Sydney and moved into Alberts premises in Rangers Road, Neutral Bay.

Reg James was the sole surviving member of the old team. John Woodward had resigned to pursue his own freelance productions for the Commonwealth Education Department. Noreen Tweeddale, reluctant to move, had also resigned.

Other changes were underway, subtly at first. The company name was now simply Gibson Productions.

THE radio industry awarded Grace the Grand Pater in 1985. She received the award from Sir Charles Moses, the former general manager of the ABC and one of Australia's pioneering radio cricket commentators.

As she travelled to the Opera House for the ceremony, Grace confided to Reg James that many years ago Sir Charles had tried to seduce her in his office. James was speechless. "I found it hard to imagine and took it with a grain of salt." But when they went backstage the first person they encountered was the very elderly Sir Charles, who awkwardly walked across to Grace and said, "Gracie, how lovely to see you. I remember the last time we met I tried to seduce you." For the second time in an hour, James was lost for words.

Grace's eightieth birthday was celebrated at James's house in Pymble. Old staff and friends surrounded her. The Yeldhams attended. Yeldham had several series running on TV and Grace frequently rang him afterwards with her comments. "Oh, Peter, I don't know that I would have accepted that…" Sparring with writers had always been one of her favourite pastimes; sadly though, her first writer-director Lynn Foster had died that year.

In a press interview to mark her birthday, Grace's Texan twang was described as "still as strong, and her fast-draw opinions still as formidable, as when she first arrived here". Asked if she considered herself the architect of Australian radio drama, she demurred: "That's very flattering, but let's just say I did some lucky things and the luckiest was coming to Australia when I did." In fact Grace had often given thought to becoming an Australian citizen, but those Texan roots were too deep. It was a step she would never take.

Grace had always been a gregarious creature, and loved nothing more than a gathering of old friends. Alastair Duncan, Nigel Lovell and some other actors clubbed together and took Grace out for a treat to City Tatts. Her parting words were, "Really, I must do this for you…" It was the last time they would see her.

GRACE was not religious in the conventional sense, and certainly her tough exterior masked any religious sentiment. The fact that she started going to St Stephens after Ronnie's death told a different story. "She did believe in God," said Reg James. "She was a Methodist."

In 1986 her brother Calvin had become very ill, yet his suicide was totally unexpected. Calvin had gone about it quietly. He had left a note for his wife on the kitchen table, warning her not to go into the garage and instructing her to call the police. He did not want to be a burden for her, nor did he want her to find his body. He was found slumped inside the car with the engine running, a hose connected to the exhaust pipe.

Grace was shattered. She asked James and his wife to accompany her to St Stephens. Grace wanted them to join her and say a prayer of what they thought at the time. Afterwards, they had their wake for Calvin at the American Club.

News of another death would follow in October — Lyndall Barbour, who had played Portia Manning all those years, succumbed to cancer at the age of 70.

IN 1987 the company's name was changed again. As The Radio Shop it would become an all-purpose production and programme distribution company. James rang Grace who was holidaying at Surfers Paradise. She was horrified and hurt. "Hell, every disc in that place has my name on it."

The company was still selling the old shows, still making money, but in addition it launched a midnight-to-dawn programming service by satellite. "But the fundamental pricing didn't appeal to stations like 4WK Toowoomba, for example," explained Reg James. "It would cost them $12 to $15 an hour. At $72 a night, that meant paying over $2,100 a month to have programming 24 hours, a huge cost for a country station that wouldn't get advertising to support it." 2UE sold a similar product for $3 an hour.

GRACE received the Order of Australia in 1987. James had gone behind the scenes and hurried through the nomination. Sir Alexis Albert had written a letter in support of the award, and so had Des Foster, president of the Federation of Australian Radio Broadcasters.

Grace rang James with the news on the Queen's Birthday Weekend. She was amazed. James recalled, "She had no sense of her own importance in the industry. And gender wasn't an issue for Grace. Sometimes I think she didn't know what she was, she didn't know there was a difference between women and men."

In November, Di Morrissey from the *Daily Telegraph* interviewed her:

> An elegant 82, she glides through her glamorous penthouse at Kings Cross wearing a turquoise caftan, jewels flashing, but an impish smile outshines the sparklers. Amid the tranquillity of Chinese antiques and amazing harbour panoramas from terrace and tall windows, it's easy to forget the sleaze of the streets below. Manicured hands nurse her Scotch and soda and you swiftly see why this woman has been so successful … charm, humour and a streak of native American practicality and get-up-and-go … This is Big Mamma when it comes to radio in this country.

Ronnie was never far from Grace's thoughts, and she told Morrissey: "Marrying Ronnie was the best thing that ever happened to me. Sadly, we never had any children."

LONG stays in St Luke's followed. Grace had a private nurse. "She was just waiting to die," said Reg James.

Ross Napier called by at the penthouse with a copy of the novel he had written. It was about a golfer, but to Grace it was full of sex and bad language; she didn't enjoy it.

Napier reflected: "She was the greatest bitch. And that was the peculiar part about it. You spent your life cursing her, but she was a woman you respected for some reason. I didn't do badly from her, it was a fairly happy arrangement, and she did become a little more generous. But she *was* bloody tight…"

Recalling his last visit, Napier said: "She wasn't well at that stage. She didn't have much left to keep her going. It was rather sad. But she remained an awesome character right to the end. No matter how far gone she was, she could still have put the fear of God into you without too much trouble. When she went, she went fairly quickly."

ON 10 July 1989, the Texan who had cast her spell over her adopted land died peacefully.

Noreen Tweeddale found her dead in bed and rang Reg James with the news. "I'd seen her three weeks before, and it was obvious she was going down," he recalled. But Tweeddale's next words left him stunned. Grace had asked that the number of people at her funeral be restricted and had left a list of whom should attend; only six names were on the list. She did not want Ross Napier invited, nor did she want Reg's wife Neryl to attend.

When the initial shock wore off, James realized why Grace had made that list. "I think she might have been afraid that nobody would want to come, and rather than risk that, she made that stipulation. I was disappointed, I must admit, but if that was her wish, then that was it."

James had wanted her to have a bigger funeral, more in accordance with her contribution to radio. Instead it was a very quiet service at the crematorium. He rang one of the radio stations, 2GB, but she had been out of the public eye for a long time. The media were not interested. "It was a shame. Her funeral should have been a real Grace Gibson Production."

Val Vine was at work when Tweeddale called her. "We knew Grace was very ill, but then Grace had been ill quite a lot of her life on and off. Some people thought she was a bit doctor-happy. Grace used to take to her bed for a couple of days and then she'd be fine." Ten minutes later, Tweeddale was on the phone again. "'Val, about the funeral… it's going to be very small and very selective.' Grace had made out a list of who could go to her funeral and for a horrible moment I thought she was trying to tell me I couldn't attend, but my name was included. It was very distressing and it was something I found very difficult to understand. It was so unexpected and so far removed from her lifestyle.

She'd been very social, on a lot of committees, gone to big parties, but to turn around at the end and have a little, dark, secretive funeral. It broke my heart." It was made more harrowing by the fact that her son could not attend. "Grace had opened her arms to the young people. He had a great love for his godmother, so it distressed him. He's never really gotten over that. Nobody will ever know what was going on in Grace's mind."

John Woodward was allowed to attend, but not his wife Betty. She, too, found it odd. "They didn't want many people there, so I thought, well, if that's the way they want it…"

Grace's great-nephew was living in Sydney when she died, and there was speculation that he had had a hand in the funeral arrangements. As it turned out, while the staff numbers had been restricted, socialities attended freely.

DINAH Shearing was saddened by the news. "I never felt that Grace was a great friend or anything, and I think she used people a little bit, and I was one of the ones, but I felt a sinking feeling because she had been part of all our pasts, she had seemed indomitable, you could never imagine her being ill. I had an affection for Grace, and I was terribly grateful for the work she put my way over the years, but on the other hand there was something aggressive about her, and so unfeeling for the people who worked for her. I was terribly frightened of her when I first started working for her, especially as I'd lied about my age to get the job. I thought she was a bit of a virago and I was scared of her."

Peter Yeldham was saddened that her old friends weren't able to celebrate her life after she died. "She should have had a lot of publicity. It was wrong that she didn't."

Val Vine believed Grace was a private person, and maybe it was as simple as that. "I think she was a lot sicker than we all thought. The world lost a lovely lady. It broke our hearts. Grace wasn't easy to get to know. I had a lot of respect for her right till the end of her life."

Alan White believed Grace was one of a kind. "She was a unique mixture of 'audience ear' — in knowing what the listeners would like, which was basically what she would like — and she was a producer of the highest standard. She had to have the very best. It just had to be right. Everything that went out under her name was one hundred per cent." White believed Grace had had a very happy life, running her company her way and following her instincts. "She also had a wonderfully happy life with her husband Ronnie. They were made for each other. Her life was fulfilled."

GRACE's great-nephew inherited the penthouse and put it on the market immediately. James went to the auction; having been there at the beginning, he wanted to be there at the end. It was sold for $1.1 million. "By that time, the art deco Macleay Regis had become an unpretentious building. In fact, many of the apartments on the lower floors were dark and dingy. It was only the penthouse and the upper floor units that would have been worthwhile buying."

The June Mendoza portrait went back to the States with Grace's great-nephew.

ALBERTS had decided to divest itself of its broadcasting interests. In 1991 they sold what was left of "Gibson's" to Bruce Ferrier's Independent Radio Services.

In 1979 Ferrier had headed 2GB/Macquarie's Special Events service, later converting it into a programme feature producer specialising in big name presenters such as Dr James Wright, Bruce Bond, and David Koch, and comedies like *The Boys from Benalla*. In 1982, he set up his own company, Independent Radio Services, producing such iconic comedy series as *How Green Was My Cactus*. (This show has recently overtaken the ABC's *Blue Hills* as Australia's longest radio feature in continuous production.) Ferrier's specialty was Australian comedy, while Gibson's was drama. It was a good fit.

"He'd talked to me before," said Reg James. "I agreed to go with Gibson's if Bruce bought it."

The first thing Ferrier did was to revive the name Grace Gibson Radio Productions. At last, Grace was back in the phone book.

Two weeks after Ferrier took over, James had a bypass operation. It was time to slow down. He now acts as a consultant, and advises clients on which shows to choose from the old library.

Even today, Grace's greatest serials — *Dossier on Dumetrius*, *Cattleman* and *Castlereagh Line* — are still being broadcast in Australia and overseas. And, more importantly, they are still being enjoyed.

Many of Grace's shows are now available on CD for private listening. Bruce Ferrier invites lovers of radio drama to purchase personal copies of their favourite shows from the Grace Gibson Radio Shop. Telephone **02 9906 2244**, write to PO Box 7377, Leura NSW, 2780, or log onto http://www.gracegibsonradio.com.

AFTER a lifetime with the company, and having listened to virtually every episode of every show, James had no hesitation in ranking the top programmes and performers:

Programmes
Dossier on Dumetrius
Cattleman
Castlereagh Line
Night Beat
Dragnet
For the Defence
Medical File
The Bishop's Mantle
Till the End of Time

Tales of the Supernatural

Top performances
Alan White, *Night Beat*
Michael Pate, *The Bishop's Mantle*
Frank Waters, *Dragnet* and *Cattleman*
Bruce Stewart, *Dossier on Dumetrius*
Dinah Shearing, *Dr Paul* and *Tudor Queen*
Richard Meikle and John Unicomb, *Becket*
Amber Mae Cecil, *Desiree*
Lloyd Lamble, *The Shadow*
Lyndall Barbour, *Portia Faces Life* and *Cattleman*
Ron Roberts, for being Ron

For the most memorable performance in a role, James singled out Thelma Scott in *Knock at the Door*, from the *Nyal Radio Playhouse*.

RADIO drama was arguably the world's shortest-lived art form. It had burned brightly for three decades, touched the lives of millions, flickered, and been extinguished. Through it all, Grace Gibson, one of its greatest exponents, had only one concern — to tell entertaining stories. The fact that generations of listeners can still remember her shows, and the characters within them, and the voices and music that brought them to life, suggests that she succeeded mightily.

www.ingramcontent.com/pod-product-compliance
Lightning Source LLC
Chambersburg PA
CBHW031426150426
43191CB00006B/418